The Truth About Burnout

The Truth About Burnout

How Organizations Cause Personal Stress and What to Do About It

Christina Maslach
Michael P. Leiter

Jossey-Bass Publishers
San Francisco

Jossey-Bass books and products are available through most bookstores. To contact Jossey-Bass directly, call (888) 378-2537, fax to (800) 605-2665, or visit our website at www.josseybass.com.

Substantial discounts on bulk quantities of Jossey-Bass books are available to corporations, professional associations, and other organizations. For details and discount information, contact the special sales department at Jossey-Bass.

Manufactured in the United States of America on acid-free paper.

Library of Congress Cataloging-in-Publication Data

Maslach, Christina.
      The truth about burnout : how organizations cause personal stress
and what to do about it / Christina Maslach, Michael P. Leiter.
            p.   cm.
      Includes bibliographical references and index.
      ISBN 0-7879-0874-6
      1. Job stress.   2. Work—Psychological aspects.   3. Stress
management.   4. Corporate culture.   I. Leiter, Michael P.
II. Title.
HF5548.85.M373   1997
158.7'2—DC21   97-21671

FIRST EDITION
HB Printing   10 9 8 7 6 5 4 3

Contents

To the very special people in our life,
who keep our engagement high
and burnout low

Phil, Zara, and Tanya
Fran, Nicola, and Sasha

Preface

The path that led to this book began with a chance telephone call many years ago. Michael wanted to spend his sabbatical year in California, and he wanted to do some new work on the phenomenon of burnout. Christina was doing research on burnout, and she happened to be in California. So the call was made, the visit was arranged, and a beautiful friendship and professional association began.

During that first year, we conducted research with the nursing staff in an HMO and also revised the Maslach Burnout Inventory, which is the measure we and other researchers have used in subsequent studies of job burnout. But after that year our work was carried out in different countries at opposite ends of the North American continent. We stayed in touch, exchanged papers, and met up occasionally at professional meetings to share our latest thinking about burnout.

At one of these conferences, however, we did more than just the usual updating—we began a new collaboration. Our shared work on burnout has encompassed new directions in theory, research, and application. And as we worked together we began to talk about the possibility, someday in the future, of writing a book.

Then chance stepped in again. Or rather, Alan Rinzler of Jossey-Bass stepped in, and he told us that we should indeed write a book, but that we should do it *now*. And with his guidance, we have done just that.

There is a special timeliness about this book—it is not the one we would have written several years ago. At that time we would have concentrated on the human services, where burnout has always been a serious concern. Today, as a result of changing economic times, burnout has become more widespread and is a major issue in more occupations, so we have expanded our focus and analysis of the phenomenon. Several years ago it would have taken us much longer to write the book together, as distance would have forced us to rely on "snail mail" and limited telephone conversations. Now, the technology of the Internet has enabled us to carry out ongoing discussions and daily rewrites of each other's drafts. We have had a few intensely productive face-to-face meetings both in California and Canada, but most of our collaboration has been mediated by the computer screen.

We knew that writing a book would involve a lot of hard work, but we didn't anticipate just how much fun it would be. The process of developing a new framework for understanding burnout and a new style of communicating it has proven to be wonderfully rewarding for both of us. In fact, we have successfully followed our own advice to build engagement with our own work.

Unlike our other projects, where there has been an important supporting cast of colleagues and staff and students and research participants, this particular project has involved just the two of us. However, our work over the years has been influenced by the contributions of many colleagues, in particular, Wilmar Schaufeli of Utrecht University in the Netherlands and Susan Jackson of New York University. We are grateful for their continuing advice, wisdom, and friendship. Michael is also thankful for the support he has received since 1982 from the Social Sciences and Humanities Research Council of Canada for his work on burnout.

But the person who was most critical in making this book a reality is Alan Rinzler, our editor. His constant encouragement, good humor, and amazingly swift feedback on everything we wrote pushed us ever onward. We learned much and accomplished more than we had expected, and we thank him for giving us that. Alan, it was a joy to work with you!

August 1997   Christina Maslach
San Francisco, California

Michael P. Leiter
Wolfville, Nova Scotia

The Truth About Burnout

1

The Current Crisis

Burnout is reaching epidemic proportions among North American workers today. It's not so much that something has gone wrong with us but rather that there have been fundamental changes in the workplace and the nature of our jobs. The workplace today is a cold, hostile, demanding environment, both economically and psychologically. People are emotionally, physically, and spiritually exhausted. The daily demands of the job, the family, and everything in between erode their energy and enthusiasm. The joy of success and the thrill of achievement are more and more difficult to attain. Dedication and commitment to the job are fading. People are becoming cynical, keeping their distance, trying not to let themselves get too involved.

This phenomenon represents a major setback on the road toward a better work life. Over the past century and a half, the workplace has progressed toward an ideal of community, away from the abusive exploitation of the mills and mines of the Industrial Revolution. In nineteenth-century factories, workers were seen as cogs in machines, easily replaced. They worked themselves into early graves. Considerable effort forced exploitative labor practices to end and built workplaces in which workers could reasonably expect some job satisfaction.

The fruits of those efforts are now at risk. The *idea* of the workplace as an efficient machine is returning to undermine the *ideal* of the workplace as a safe and healthy setting in which people may fulfill their potential through intrinsically rewarding work for which they are given fair compensation.

HOW THE WORKPLACE HAS CHANGED

What has happened to bring on this crisis? Why is burnout becoming a more common part of our vocational vocabulary? Why are well-intentioned workers, managers, and community leaders unable to do anything about it? The problem's roots lie in economic trends, technology, and management philosophy.

Less Intrinsic Worth

Particularly damaging to the community of the workplace is that organizations are cashing in their intrinsic worth. Instead of providing a foundation for research and long-term growth, corporations are cashing in their assets for short-term stock performance. Borrowed money fuels the frantic pace of mergers and acquisitions among international corporations. The scope of this activity leaves companies leveraged out of all proportion on a foundation of debt. Because of this enormous and constant pressure, these organizations' first priority is to generate cash flow to service their debts, not to create excellent products or build a stronger community. The latter become the local concerns of the people within these organizations, while the larger system looks merely to manage finances.

The absence of concern for product or people turns the rationale for a corporation inside out. Rather than corporations existing to extend the capacity of people to earn a living and make significant accomplishments, people are sacrificing their livelihoods and their aspirations for the good of the corporation. Work has become an obligation rather than a resource. The values that determine the quality of organizational life are not those of cohesive work groups attempting to provide excellent products or services but those of bottom-line management in an entity that is desperate for cash flow. More problematic still, major corporations are beyond the control of local communities. Their considerable economic and political clout eclipses anything that might be happening within a community.

Global Economics

Manufacturing work is moving out of the community and out of the country. Rapid transportation and communication allow work to go anywhere, and so work is going to where the cost of doing business is cheaper. Governments in industrialized nations have reduced the trade barriers that protected their higher-cost local industries partly because of pressure from powerful multinational corporations and partly because old-style protectionist policies simply do not work anymore. In consequence, workers in North America, Australia, and Europe find themselves competing with workers in developing countries.

This competition is affecting an ever-widening range of the economy. At first, only rudimentary work could be moved to developing countries. Their people did not have the skills necessary for complex manufacturing jobs; their industrial support systems—roads, telephone systems, electrical power—were inadequate to support major industries. Now, all that is changing. Workers in developing countries are becoming more capable because they are getting better educations. At the same time, technological advances in production are simplifying manufacturing jobs so that less technical know-how is required. And industrial support systems are improving, especially near borders and major seaports. As these trends converge, more developing nations can provide corporations with the workers they need to begin production. Although the labor remains much cheaper, it is adequate for a wider range of jobs.

Consequently, entire industries have disappeared from developed countries. What has gone offshore? Everything, including the kitchen sink. In 1995 Pfister Faucets, the largest U.S. maker of faucets, closed down its Pacoima, California, manufacturing operation and laid off 550 workers while opening a plant in Mexico.[1] Hundreds of thousands of other manufacturing jobs—making shoes, clothing, toys, and computers—have also moved offshore. The South Carolina textile industry employed 148,800 in 1970 but only 90,800 in 1995.[2] In computer manufacturing, jobs did not so much move offshore as develop offshore in the first place during the explosive growth of the industry over the past two decades.

The possibility of moving jobs out of the country puts pressure on those who remain. The Brookings Institute reports that a number of U.S. corporations have moved a majority of their assets out of the country: Gillette (66 percent), Mobil (63 percent), IBM (55 percent), Bankers Trust (52 percent), and Citicorp (51 percent). By 1995 half of Xerox's one hundred thousand employees worked outside of the United States. As Edith Holleman, former counsel to the House Science, Space, and Technology Committee and its Investigations and Oversight Subcommittee, said in a speech at a major engineering conference, "Nissan, Texas Instruments, and Xerox have state-of-the-art facilities in Aguascalientes, Mexico, employing tens of thousands of Mexicans. But they don't share the profits of their work. Most of them live in slums with two telephones for twenty thousand people." In response to a 1994 incident in which someone sent a bomb through Xerox's interoffice mail, Xerox spokesperson Tom Abbott said, "Xerox employees are under a tremendous amount of stress and pressure as a result of the reduction in workforce. They are losing their friends and co-workers and know they have to deal with more work with less people. Let's put it this way: We're all being very cautious."[3]

The wage savings gained through these moves are considerable. The Kirkwood Company produces electronic components for a variety of appliance manufacturers—including Philips, Braun, and Sunbeam—at a Mexican plant where wages range from U.S.$2.23 to U.S.$6.15 a day; these jobs would pay over $10 an hour in the United States. Meanwhile, the average hourly wage of nonsupervisory workers in the United States declined 11 percent between 1978 and 1995, down to $11.46 despite increased productivity.

Wage concessions are not the whole story. A more enduring impact is on the quality of the work life itself. Workers are conceding their time. They are working longer hours. They are taking work home, often continuing after hours on computer equipment they have purchased themselves. They are devoting more time to tasks that are not personally rewarding, that is, that are not enjoyable and do not further their careers. They are even giving up long-cherished benefits, like fully paid health insurance and company-financed pension plans.

Globalization highlights the weak points in the economic systems of industrialized nations by increasing competitive pressures. In contrast, without competitive pressure, large corporations and governments can delay addressing programs that either do not work or operate inefficiently. Competitive pressures put an end to those practices, but do not necessarily improve things. In pushing for efficiency, competitive pressures make corporations myopic. They cut costs in the short term at the expense of programs and policies that would make sense in the long run.

Technology

How do corporations get the work done with fewer people who are feeling more anxious and making less money? The two general strategies for enhancing productivity are to use sophisticated technology and tight human resource management.

Sophisticated technology can replace jobs entirely. Elevators and switchboards used to have operators, now they are automated. Banking machines reduce the ranks of tellers around the world. Robots replace assembly workers because machines can do some tasks much faster and more accurately than people can.

The impact of technology is not being felt solely in the technical and manufacturing sectors. Automation is making inroads in the information sector. Government agencies are replacing employment counselors with interactive information kiosks. Distance education centers, such as the one at Arizona State University, are putting high school and university courses onto CD-ROMs. People are receiving counseling and education services without making direct contact with other people. Downsizing in these sectors has decreased the personal qualities of these services. Many people prefer interacting with a computer to enduring a long wait to speak with an overworked employment counselor. Indeed, students note that distance education provides as much if not more personal contact with an instructor than do huge lecture classes.

Machines often do jobs that are not very attractive. The problem is that the worker who is relieved of drudgery is also relieved of a job. Furthermore, the technology changes faster than people can learn new skills. So when the company uses machines, it becomes more productive but many individuals lose income, positions, and opportunities for training.

For those who continue working, technology brings new demands. Take a moment to think about it. How many passwords do you have to remember? How often do computer crashes interrupt your work? How much time do you spend backing up your work? How often do you wish you had spent more time backing up your work? How much time do you spend sorting through e-mail? How much of the operating budget at your workplace goes to the purchase of computers, software, and maintenance services? The power of technology is paid for in both time and money. There are days when people doubt whether information technology really increases productivity or merely rearranges how they spend their time.

Redistribution of Power

The second strategy for increasing productivity is tight human resource management.

The power of unions is weakening. Their members are becoming less willing to put their jobs on the line as they lose confidence in the possibility of obtaining better wages and greater job security. From 1980 to 1990 the number of manufacturing jobs in the United States dropped by 5 percent, or roughly one million jobs.[4]

Even more important, highly skilled union jobs decreased considerably to be replaced by low-skilled, minimum wage, nonunion jobs. The unions that replaced professional associations among teachers, nurses, and university professors in the 1970s and 1980s have similarly lost clout. These unions are perceived as slowing down the organization's response to outside pressures. Overwhelmed by these kinds of pressures, the traditional union power base is eroding.

At the same time, tight human resource management—or micromanagement—has become the order of the day, with policies that focus employees on the bottom line. But the employees, especially those who have been through graduate or professional programs, put other values first. Health care providers in HMOs are frustrated by policies that prescribe treatments. Teachers feel constrained by curriculum standards established by legislation, such as Goals 2000. (To improve the accountability of educators, this legislation constrains the extent to which teachers, parents, students, and local administrators control the educational system.) Middle managers feel constrained by dictates from central management and regulatory agencies.

In all of these examples, the central authority within the organization is reducing the prerogatives of professionals and front-line managers, making these people less responsive to local conditions. The restrictions also affect these individuals' sense of efficacy because they diminish their capacity to control what occurs in their work. Despite the many management books and seminars that proclaim empowerment to be the trend, people in organizations feel more constrained. In practice, problems are delegated but the power to address them is not.

Failing Corporate Citizenship

As the tenets of good corporate citizenship erode, people find it difficult to commit themselves to the organizations where they work. While the front-line staff work harder in more tenuous positions for less compensation, senior personnel do very well. Downsizing causes short-term increases in the stock price, which affect CEOs indirectly through their salary and directly through the stockholdings that make up an ever increasing proportion of their compensation packages in the United States. A few extreme examples follow.

As part of a merger with Kimberly-Clark in 1995, Al Dunlap walked away from his twenty-month job as CEO of Scott Paper with $100 million in compensation; his three top lieutenants received over $15 million each. Dunlap's contribution to the company was cutting its research spending in half, eliminating staff training programs, and laying off a third of his thirty-three thousand employees. As one commentator stated, "Dunlap didn't create value. He redistributed income from the employees and the community to the shareholders."[5]

The movement of jobs from the United States to Mexico contributes to this situation. A recent report from the Institute for Policy Studies noted that, in 1994, while U.S. wages remained constant and the value of Mexican wages dropped because of the devaluation of the peso, CEOs gave themselves pay raises averaging 30 percent. For example, Lawrence Bossidy, CEO of Allied Signal, received a $12.4 million salary—nearly double the combined annual salaries of his thirty-eight hundred Mexican workers.[6]

It's not that these companies are doing so well under these CEOs. William Agee of the Morrison Knudsen Corporation resigned in 1995 at the end of a year in which the company lost $114 million and 277 workers were laid off. Agee received $3.5 million for his performance that year.

Similarly, Robert Allen, CEO of AT&T, received $5.2 million in compensation the year he announced the layoff of forty thousand employees and AT&T barely broke even. The resulting bad press he received prompted him to write an open letter to all AT&T employees justifying his salary (which he reported to be $2.7 million) as modest compensation in light of his responsibilities, and justifying the low profits as the result of major capital investments that were intended to keep AT&T globally competitive. He discounted altogether the value of his stock options, asserting that they were worthless unless AT&T's stock price met ambitious target levels in 1999.[7]

This final point is not a cause for reassurance. By linking a CEO's potential for vast wealth to stock values, a company can damage its own long-term potential to grow and contribute to society. Such links encourage CEOs to exploit the intrinsic value of corporations for personal gain. The situation in which U.S. corporations now find themselves has parallels in the Soviet Union's domination of Central Europe after World War II, when that country exploited the wealth of those nations to maintain an economic system that was not viable. CEOs today are being rewarded for cashing in the existing value of corporations rather than for building new value.

The problem is most evident in the United States, where the average remuneration for executives is roughly double that in Europe and Japan. In 1974, top U.S. CEOs got 35 times the average industrial wage; by 1994, this ratio had jumped to 187 times the pay of average workers. In Europe, the ratio is less than twenty to one.[8] Furthermore, this contrast is not only evident among the highest-paid CEOs. Average U.S. CEOs earn twenty-four times the average industrial wage; in Canada, the ratio is twelve to one, and in Northern Europe it is generally less than ten to one. The extremely high earnings of CEOs do not appear to be just compensation for a valuable contribution. There is little evidence that CEOs are quitting because of insufficient compensation, so it seems unlikely that such extreme salaries are necessary to keep them on the job. In this kind of job climate, how can one blame employees for losing confidence that organizations are fair, considerate communities?

WHY BURNOUT IS THRIVING

In the current climate, burnout thrives in the workplace. Burnout is always more likely when there is a major mismatch between the nature of the job and the nature of the person who does the job. Increasingly, we work in job settings in which human values place a distant second behind economic ones. What makes us tick as human beings, what inspires us to work well in addition to working hard, is ignored or played down. We are supposed to adjust to the demands of this brave new world and figure out how to survive in it. But when the gap between people and the demands of the job is so great, this progress comes at a high human price. We experience this mismatch in a number of areas of organizational life.

We Feel Overloaded

Eleanor works in an insurance company that has been trying to make budget cuts by downsizing through attrition for the most part, although Eleanor once found herself in the painful position of having to lay off one of her own staff members. With fewer employees overall, the caseloads of those remaining have increased to the extent where they cannot effectively serve their clients or adequately scrutinize questionable claims.

"I try to be sympathetic with the staff when they discuss the impossibility of managing the workload, but I just don't have any room to maneuver. I tell them, 'I know it's a lousy way to work, but we all have to make do and be productive or our department will be closed.' I'm convinced that if I don't meet the next cost-reduction objective or if I stop putting in extra time, I will be in the next group of employees to lose their jobs. So I'm always anxious and tense and irritable. And constantly exhausted—even before I go to work, when I'm trying to get the kids off to school. And I feel so guilty about how little time I'm spending with my family—I've put off our vacation twice. I don't think I can keep up this pace forever, but right now I don't see an alternative."

Work overload is perhaps the most obvious indication of a mismatch between the person and the job. We have to do too much in too little time with too few resources. It is a matter not of stretching to meet new challenges but of going far beyond human limits. Downsizing in an organization rarely includes reducing its mandate, so fewer people have to get the same amount of work done in less time. The pace increases further as people take on a second job or moonlight on the side in an attempt to meet financial pressures and keep their job options open.

Work overload is increasing as the tempo of work increases. The faster pace hurts quality, disrupts collegial relationships, kills innovation—and brings on burnout.

We Lack Control over What We Do

Stan is a psychologist who started his career as an eager, open-minded, caring person who wanted to help others. He was the kind of therapist most people would want to see if they were struggling with problems. But gradually Stan has become a cynical, frustrated individual who feels he is losing control over his job—financially, professionally, and ethically—and he's beginning to want out.

"There is no joy in it any longer. I hate it. After a day of dealing with clients' pain, I'm exhausted and just don't want to be with people anymore. Clients expect me to be there twenty-four hours a day and get upset if they get a recorded message instead. And the managed care system is making it worse. I no longer have control over the type and quality of care I provide—some reviewer in some company who doesn't know the client and who has less training than I do decides how many sessions I can have. All that matters is keeping costs down, not what's good for the client, and it's really hard to live with that. Sometimes I lie so I can get more care, but it's hard to live with that too. And even though I am working more hours than ever, I am getting paid less. This is a life?"

Lack of control over one's work is another important indication that the person and the job are mismatched. People want the opportunity to make choices and decisions, use their ability to think and solve problems, and have some input in the process of achieving the outcomes for which they will be held accountable. There is a world of difference between being accountable and being constrained by rigid policies and tight monitoring.

Policies that take a narrow, cookie-cutter, one-size-fits-all approach don't allow much room for people to improve or innovate, and as a result they feel less responsible for the outcomes, not more. Mechanical management leads to mechanical performance. Similarly, close monitoring of staff performance has a human cost beyond the supervisor's time and energy in that it diminishes the capacity of staff members to adapt and take the initiative. This kind of monitoring sends the message that "you can't be trusted, we don't respect your judgment, you aren't very smart, you are incapable of doing this by yourself." This kind of message should never be given to young children and when it is given to adults, it's equally demeaning.

We Are Not Rewarded for Our Work

As a public school teacher, John has the challenge of teaching history to classes filled with thirty-five to forty rambunctious thirteen-year-olds.

"Teaching requires a lot of energy, and you have to be *on* all the time—so you don't sit down, you don't have time to take a break or eat lunch because you're still working with kids who need extra time and attention, you don't go to the bathroom when you need to—it's high stress all the time. You'd think we would be entitled to extra 'combat pay!' Instead, we get an abysmally low salary for an 'eight-hour workday'—which is a real joke, given how many nonbillable hours I have to spend after school meeting with parents or attending meetings or supervising extracurricular activities, and then spending evenings and weekends grading and preparing lesson plans.

"When people hear that I am a teacher, they say things like 'I feel sorry for you' or 'Why would you want to spend your time with adolescents all day long?' Even the students pick up on it. 'Why are you a teacher, when you don't make as much money as my dad?' they say. I still believe it's an important job, but it gets hard when students don't make the effort to study or do homework, and when parents constantly complain that you haven't given *their* child special attention, or that the child's failings are all your fault, not theirs."

Lack of reward for contributions on the job is a third mismatch between job and person. When we don't get recognition, both the work we do and we ourselves as workers are devalued. Although everyone knows that rewards are important, this knowledge does not necessarily translate into action. Monetary rewards are easy to administer and are usually well received, but money is tight these days (except, as we saw earlier, for executives at the top). Instead of enjoying financially rewarding careers, people endure the doldrums of wage freezes, the anxiety of short-term jobs, and the purgatory of slow payment for contract work. Managers are just as busy as the people they manage. Since expanded responsibilities are the result of widespread gutting of middle management, managers oversee more people but have less time to keep track of them. Most devastating for workers, however, is the loss of the internal reward that comes when a person takes pride in doing something of importance and value to others, and doing that job well.

We're Experiencing a Breakdown in Community

Martha works as a hospital laboratory technologist. A vibrant community just a few years ago, the hospital is now the scene of endless political intrigues that are the result of downsizing and rumors of a complete closure. Although Martha has an impressive range of skills and experience, she has problems with management and feels alienated from the job. She would like to get out entirely but no opportunities look promising, so she keeps her distance from the work and everyone around her.

"I feel the new lab manager is a real detriment to the laboratory. The lab techs have very little say in the workings of the laboratory and therefore feel they have little control over their jobs or the quality of care they can provide. There is no rapport or respect between the technologists and the manager. Many of us are afraid of him, and I feel he encourages this kind of management by intimidation. Because there's no communication, rumors are always abundant and people are left to assume things or make the wrong conclusions. The techs keep their mouths shut at meetings, and problems persist while everybody tries to keep their asses covered."

Lack of community is the result when people lose a positive connection with others in the workplace. People thrive in community, and they function best when praise, comfort, happiness, and humor are shared with others they like and respect. But sometimes the job isolates people: they may be physically separated, they may spend most of their time with computers, or they may be just too busy to get together. Sometimes technology makes social contact impersonal—when people have to communicate with machines (like answering machines and voice mail systems) rather than with a live human being, for example. Sometimes the job has a chilling effect on what people can say or do because of explicit or implicit prohibitions, such as those brought about by concerns about political correctness or the threat of litigation.

However, what is most destructive to a sense of community is chronic and unresolved conflict. Conflict infuses the workplace with frustration, anger, fear, anxiety, disrespect, and suspicion. It tears apart the fabric of social support, making it less likely that people will help each other out when times get tough.

We Aren't Treated Fairly

Bill is the network manager at a university, and it is his responsibility to keep the computer network up and running. But it's not a very good computer system and, consequently, is prone to crashing.

"This morning I managed to revive it after being beeped at 5:30 A.M. Then at 8:30 I had to waste an hour and a half at the User Support Implementation Group meeting listening to academics and administrators tell me that the current level of performance is 'unacceptable.' Of course it's unacceptable! I told them two years ago that they would have problems but they vetoed my own recommendation for a UNIX operating system because they didn't want to pay for it. They were all swept away by this new operating system's bells and whistles without a clue of how unreliable this software could be. What few staff are assigned to me don't have the basic skills needed to keep things running, and as soon as they learn enough to be useful, they leave for higher salaries elsewhere—salaries higher than mine, even though they don't have a tenth of my ability.

"Unfortunately, I'm stuck here for two more years until my wife finishes her graduate degree. But then I'm gone. The icing on the cake came this afternoon when the public relations office told me I was going to receive the university's Quality Through Technological Innovation Award. I told them to stuff it."

Lack of fairness in the workplace is a serious mismatch between people and the job environment. Fairness in the workplace means that people are shown respect and their self-worth is confirmed. Mutual respect among people who work together is at the heart of any sense of community. We lose trust in an organization that shows no fairness, because this implies that those in authority are not honest and do not respect who we are. Unfairness is most evident during the evaluation and promotion processes. But day-to-day interactions may also be unfair—when people get blamed for things they didn't do, for example.

Lack of fairness is also evident when there is inequity of workload or pay, or when people bend the rules or cheat in order to get ahead. And if procedures for grievance or dispute resolution don't allow both parties to have a voice, the procedures will be judged unfair. At a larger level, organizational policies that send the message that money takes precedence over employees causes mutual respect and shared values to erode.

We're Dealing with Conflicting Values

Steve is a loan officer in a small-town bank, a job that he sees as a way to make a meaningful contribution to his community. People come to him at crucial decision points in their lives: when they buy a house or a car, renovate their property, or experience a downturn in their fortunes that requires restructuring their expenses and their debts. Of late, critical decisions made by the head office have strained his feelings toward the bank.

"The bank says it puts customer service first. We are supposed to be personal bankers who develop long-term relationships with our customers, are responsive to their needs, and are active in the community. Then they call us together at seminars and tell us to push products. Pushing products is incompatible with responding to customers. Products are what we have packaged to sell. Customers do not come in the door ready for a prepackaged product. They come here with problems that need unique solutions."

On a larger scale, Steve is at odds with the bank's downsizing of front-line staff in the past year while it reported record profits. This was a mean-spirited way to treat loyal staff, and it was bad for business in the long run. As Steve said to the bank's regional vice president, "I live in an agricultural region. When we have an apple tree that is not producing, we don't go out and hack away at its roots. We go to the top of the tree and prune out the dead wood."

A *value conflict* occurs when there is a mismatch between the requirements of the job and our personal principles. In some cases, a job can lead people to do things that are unethical and clash with their personal values. For example, a worker might have to tell a lie in order to make a sale, get necessary authorization, or cover up a mistake. In other cases, a worker may be caught in the organization's own conflicting values, which often reflect a discrepancy between the lofty mission statement ("We provide customer service of the highest quality") and the actual company goal ("We provide the bare minimum of service in order to keep costs down").

In all too many situations, workers operate in a Machiavellian milieu where the ends justify the means. The subsequent moral erosion can be high. People do their best when they believe in what they are doing and when they can maintain their pride, integrity, and self-respect.

THE EROSION OF THE SOUL

Burnout is the index of the dislocation between what people are and what they have to do. It represents an erosion in values, dignity, spirit, and will—an erosion of the human soul. It is a malady that spreads gradually and continuously over time, putting people into a downward spiral from which it's hard to recover.

If the experiences this chapter just described ring a bell with you, then you may be at risk for burnout. Let's assume that you are working in a situation of chronic imbalance in which the job demands more than you can give and provides less than you need. Just like the people described in the preceding paragraphs, you feel overworked, undervalued, and no longer in control of the job you do. What might happen if you begin to burn out? Actually, three things happen: you become chronically exhausted; you become cynical and detached from your work; and you feel increasingly ineffective on the job.

The Dimensions of Burnout

Let's take a closer look at each of the three dimensions of burnout.

Exhaustion. When people feel exhaustion, they feel overextended, both emotionally and physically. They feel drained, used up, and unable to unwind and recover. When they awake in the morning, they are just as tired as when they went to bed. They lack the energy to face another project or another person. Exhaustion is the first reaction to the stress of job demands or major change.

Cynicism. When people feel cynical, they take a cold, distant attitude toward work and the people on the job. They minimize their involvement at work and even give up their ideals. In a way, cynicism is an attempt to protect oneself from exhaustion and disappointment. People feel it may be safer to be indifferent, especially when the future is uncertain, or to assume things won't work out rather than get their hopes up. But being so negative can seriously damage a person's well-being and capacity to work effectively.

Ineffectiveness. When people feel ineffective, they feel a growing sense of inadequacy. Every new project seems overwhelming. The world seems to conspire against each of their attempts to make progress, and what little they do accomplish may seem trivial. They lose confidence in their ability to make a difference. And as they lose confidence in themselves, others lose confidence in them.

What Really Causes Burnout?

The conventional wisdom is that burnout is primarily a problem of the individual. That is, people burn out because of flaws in their characters, behavior, or productivity. According to this perspective, *people* are the problem, and the solution is to change them or get rid of them.

But our research argues most emphatically otherwise. As a result of extensive study, we believe that burnout is not a problem of the people themselves but of the *social environment* in which people work. The structure and functioning of the workplace shape how people interact with one another and how they carry out their jobs. When the workplace does not recognize the human side of work, then the risk of burnout grows, carrying a high price with it.

The High Cost of Burnout

Burnout can have a deadly impact even beyond its erosion of the soul. It can be detrimental to your health, your ability to cope, and your personal lifestyle. It can lead to a serious deterioration in your job performance. And these costs are not just yours alone—they are felt by everyone who is affected by you, both on the job and at home.

In terms of personal functioning, burnout can cause such physical problems as headaches, gastrointestinal illness, high blood pressure, muscle tension, and chronic fatigue. Burnout may lead to mental distress in the form of anxiety, depression, and sleep disturbances. To try to cope with the stress, some people increase use of alcohol and drugs. If they bring burnout home, their exhaustion and negative feelings begin to affect relationships with family and friends.

And what about the job itself? One final result of burnout's negative downward spiral is that, as they become more stressed and receive less support in their personal lives, people become even less capable of dealing with problems on the job. People who are burning out are likely to withdraw from the job, both psychologically and physically. They invest less time and energy in their work, do only what is absolutely necessary, and are absent more often. In addition to doing less, they do their work less well. High-quality work requires time and effort, commitment and creativity, but the burned-out individual is no longer willing to give these freely. The drop in quality and quantity of work produced is the occupational bottom line of burnout.

Eventually, some people reach the point where they can't take it anymore and they quit. Even when it's necessary, such a decision can be very painful if it means walking away from a career that was once a source of pride, prestige, and personal identity. As one high school teacher put it, "I've been teaching for over twenty years, but I've lost my self-confidence. I can't keep doing this, I don't *want* to keep doing this, because I don't like the values of our society as I see them in the schools—anti-learning, anti-effort, anti-responsibility. If education isn't going to make a difference, then why have I been busting my buns? I just want to go somewhere else and have a life. So I'm just in a basic survival mode now."

As you can see, the costs of burnout are significant both for people and organizations. For employees, the issue is a job that diminishes the quality of their lives and their potential for a productive, growing career. For organizations, the issue is a workforce that no longer provides the dedication, creativity, and productivity that it once did.

Burnout Then and Now

Burnout is not a new phenomenon. Twenty years ago, burnout was an issue of primary concern for workers in people-oriented occupations such as human services, health care, and education. In today's terminology, these occupations are high-touch, that is, they involve lots of face-to-face contact. Then as now, such jobs can be so emotionally and physically demanding that the risk for burnout is high. The dedication these jobs demand, the long hours and excessive workloads, are exhausting, as are potential conflicts with clients, patients, students, colleagues, or supervisors. In order to cope, some workers distance themselves from the people they come into contact with and from personal involvement in their work. Furthermore, the difficulties in achieving major successes can lead these workers to doubt their competence and to question the wisdom of sticking with this type of job.

The difference today is that more and more jobs are high-touch. For one thing, there has been an enormous shift from manufacturing to service jobs, where people have to deal effectively with their clientele and provide good customer service. And in a working world that is increasingly high-tech, high-touch becomes even more critical—customers want to be able to deal with a real human being, not just a computer.

Also, there has been growth in the number of managerial positions, in which people have to oversee employees and effectively motivate them to be productive. In addition, there has been a growing trend toward work teams, in which people have to work collaboratively with colleagues rather than on their own. Yet despite the rise on many levels of high-touch work, training in the skills to do it well is generally given short shrift. Interpersonal skills get passed over in favor of technical or economic ones. As we shall see, the

psychological costs of such work are still not recognized as an important source of job stress.

So now more than ever the workplace is fertile ground for burnout. But if we have known about burnout for some time, why haven't we figured out what to do about it? To some extent, the problem is that burnout has, as the saying goes, "gotten no respect." It has been underrated, trivialized, not taken seriously. It does not pose major risks for physical injury or death, unlike other job hazards. Chronic erosion of feelings and skills over time is not as striking as an immediate crisis. Consequently, people assume that burnout is no big deal, and they misjudge the risks. They also assume that it won't happen to them—that they are too knowledgeable or too strong to fall prey to the problem. When burnout does set in, people tend to keep working, even if not as well as before, so there are no serious threats to general productivity. Viewed from this perspective, burnout is just a cop-out, the whining of wimps who can't handle serious work and can't admit to failure. The feeling is that there is really nothing to "do" about burnout. In other words, if it ain't broke, don't fix it.

Unfortunately, this perspective is all wrong. It is short-sighted and does not take the big picture into account. This perspective is based on myths and misunderstandings about why people work and how they work.

OUR CURE FOR THE CRISIS

In this book, we argue that burnout is not a trivial problem but an important barometer of a major social dysfunction in the workplace. As such, burnout deserves serious attention. The emotional and financial costs are too high for it to be ignored or dismissed any longer.

We argue that burnout in individual workers says more about the conditions of their job than it does about them. Contrary to popular opinion, it's not the individual but the organization that needs to change, especially in the present work environment.

We argue that effective responses to burnout must involve prevention rather than just treatment. The *process* of intervention is thus more critical than any one particular solution.

We argue that greater success in coping with burnout will come from focusing on promoting engagement with work rather than from just focusing on reducing burnout. Thus, we advocate a model of organizational health that includes the promotion of human values in the workplace, rather than just economic ones.

Our arguments have a solid basis in research. We have been studying burnout for twenty years and have spoken to thousands of workers in many occupations across North America. So we think we know what we are talking about. And that is why we are challenging the accepted wisdom and proposing a better way to think about burnout.

In this book we address the crises in organizational life. We neither celebrate the changes in the nature of organizations and careers nor advocate escape from them. Organizations, especially large organizations, are here to stay for quite a while. Although their form and processes will continue to evolve with advancing technology and different economic conditions, they will remain the primary job environment for a substantial proportion of working people. We think the current crisis gives us an opportunity to address major shortcomings in organizational life, an opportunity to address the pressures leading to chronic exhaustion, cynicism, and ineffectiveness, and an opportunity to build productive engagement with work. And, most of all, it gives us an opportunity to begin closing the gaps between people and the workplace.

2

How You Experience Burnout

Ask people what it's like to feel burned out, and you're likely to hear the following:

"I'm *frustrated!* It's getting impossible to do a good job, and the situation just keeps getting worse."

"I have lost my enthusiasm for work I really liked."

"I have lots of anger, and nowhere to take it."

"I'm scared—is the job going to last?"

"I am getting more unhappy and depressed every day on the job—and questioning whether I should stick with it."

"I'm feeling overwhelmed, overloaded, overworked—and trapped. There's no way out."

Each person expresses burnout in a unique way, but the basic themes are the same:

An erosion of engagement with the job. What started out as important, meaningful, fascinating work becomes unpleasant, unfulfilling, and meaningless.

An erosion of emotions. The positive feelings of enthusiasm, dedication, security, and enjoyment fade away and are replaced by anger, anxiety, and depression.

A problem of fit between the person and the job. Individuals see this imbalance as a personal crisis, but it is really the workplace that is in trouble.

As the word *erosion* suggests, burnout is a gradual process of loss during which the mismatch between the needs of the person and the demands of the job grows ever greater. The demands of the workplace shape the individual's experience, while the individual's performance affects the workplace and all the people in it. Thus, the erosion process has something of a chicken-and-egg quality—does it begin with the person or the job?—but popular wisdom usually lays the blame on the individual.

We feel this is the wrong way to approach the problem of burnout. As we explained in Chapter One, powerful economic, political, and cultural forces are affecting the workplace, creating a climate that is more conducive than ever to burnout. It doesn't make sense for anyone to say, "I'm to blame." That kind of thinking won't help us deal with burnout. The job context is as much a part of the downward spiral as the individual is, so it needs to be a part of any solution.

AN EROSION OF ENGAGEMENT

People don't begin a job feeling burned out. At the very least they hope it will provide a steady income and some security, regardless of whether they are thrilled about the actual work itself. In the best circumstances, people begin by feeling fully engaged with their work. They feel energetic, ready to commit time and effort to the job tasks. They feel involved and find the work activities meaningful. The sense of accomplishment they gain from these activities makes them feel competent and effective.

Energy, involvement, and *efficacy*—these are the direct opposites of the three dimensions of burnout. As we described in Chapter One, when burnout begins, this sense of engagement begins to fade and there is a corresponding shift from these three positive feelings to their negative counterparts. *Energy* turns into *exhaustion, involvement* turns into *cynicism,* and *efficacy* turns into *ineffectiveness.*

The following case is a classic example of the erosion of engagement.

Julie taught history and literature to eighth graders in a public school and had a reputation as an outstanding teacher. Students loved her, parents called to get their child enrolled in her class, and the principal rated her as one of the best. Young and successful, Julie was expected to have a long and distinguished teaching career. But this year, Julie decided to quit. Her decision came as a shock to everyone; some of her colleagues cried when they heard the news.

At one time Julie was completely dedicated to the job because it allowed her to do things she valued highly—to make a difference in the world, to have a positive impact on other people's lives. But today she doesn't feel the job is worth it. At one time she brought enormous energy and commitment to her work, putting in long hours and agreeing to do all sorts of "extras" above and beyond the call of duty. Now she is exhausted just going through the motions and doing the bare minimum. At one time she was deeply involved with her students, attentive to their progress and achievement in learning, sensitive to their individual needs. Now she is more negative and cynical about their motivation and skills. At one time she was confident that her efforts would pay off, that the kids would get a better education and a better start on life because of what she and other teachers were able to accomplish. Now she questions whether the students are really getting what they need; she even worries that children are getting damaged by overworked teachers like herself. To Julie, trying to do good came at too high a price.

What is noteworthy about Julie's case, and many others like it, is that the negative slide to burnout started from a position of strength and success rather than from one of weakness. Julie was not an incompetent, lazy individual who didn't know how to teach. She brought to the job an impressive set of credentials and personal qualities and was able to use these to produce high-quality teaching. In terms of skills and motivation, she was at the top of her class—one could hardly ask for more. As one of her colleagues said,

"Julie was 'on fire' from the beginning, not like some of those teachers who never even 'light up' in the first place. She had a passion for teaching, and it is so depressing to see that disappear." Indeed, losing the best and the brightest—people like Julie—is the most devastating cost of burnout.

Six Sources of Burnout

What led to the erosion of Julie's engagement with teaching? A close look at her case reveals the presence of the six mismatches between job and person that we described in Chapter One.

Work overload was a major factor from the beginning. Julie spent intense eight-hour days in the classroom and extra hours—after school, in the evening, and on weekends—to prepare for class, grade homework, and attend meetings. Although she had a great deal of control over how she taught her class ("When I close that door, the class is all mine—just me and the kids"), she had a *lack of control* over the district policies that led to increased class sizes and decreased teaching resources. Like other teachers, she received a low salary that was clearly *insufficient reward;* she didn't mind so much when she was young and single and just starting out in the profession, but later it posed a severe financial burden. Furthermore, low salaries are the most visible symbol of the lack of respect for teaching. Julie's wages fueled her sense that there was an inherent *unfairness* in the system ("Why am I working so hard, doing so much, and yet getting so little in return?"). The bickering, political infighting, and competitiveness between the teachers in her school made her feel alienated from them, and thus there was a *breakdown of community.* Finally, there was a growing *value conflict* between what Julie was trying to achieve in the classroom and the "extras" she was being asked to do by the school. As she put it, "The last straw was when they wanted me to spend a lot of time pulling together all this material to prepare an application for a 'good school' award—there was far more concern about getting the award than actually doing the things that would make us a good school!"

AN EROSION OF EMOTIONS

What is also noteworthy about Julie's textbook case is the parallel erosion of emotion she experienced. At one time, Julie exuded energy, enthusiasm, and compassion. She had a great sense of humor and an easygoing rapport with her students. Now she describes herself as being "on edge" all the time, having a "short fuse" with the students, and feeling too exhausted to teach the intensive curriculum that used to be her forte. Anger, cynicism, and bitterness are the dominant emotions—it's as though her original passion underwent a negative transformation. These new emotions changed Julie's relationships with all the people she dealt with at school: her colleagues, the principal, the parents and, most important, her students.

The Emotional Fallout of Burnout

Frustration and anger are the emotional hallmarks of burnout. You feel frustrated because you are blocked from achieving your goals. You cannot overcome the obstacles in your path either because you lack sufficient resources to do your job or because you lack control over the work. You are not given the rewards you expect. Not surprisingly, you feel ineffective. But you also feel exhausted as a result of wasted time and effort. The anger that accompanies your frustration fuels negative reactions toward people and cynicism about the job. Because you have these negative reactions, you are likely to look for scapegoats and blame others for your problems and to respond to them more aggressively and punitively. This is especially likely if your anger has been aroused in a context that you perceive as unfair. Furthermore, if you are angry you are likely to be more rigid in how you do your work and less open to new alternatives.

Hostility is also the result when people feel humiliated or embarrassed on the job. If people aren't treated with respect and trust and if their work is not valued, their self-esteem and sense of competence are threatened. People begin to feel alienated from the workplace and may even attempt destructive acts in retaliation, such as theft or sabotage. As one worker put it, "No one gets the respect they want or feel they deserve. That's why they shoot their bosses and blow up places."

Fear and anxiety are two other negative emotions that contribute to burnout. These feelings are especially likely when people lack control over their work and when the job environment is an uncertain or threatening one. As we saw in Chapter One, this is the situation that many people face in the workplace today. Although the common wisdom is that people work better when they're in competition with others and running scared, worry about the future may actually function as a major distraction and cause them to work with less attention, energy, and commitment.

However, burnout is not just about the presence of negative emotions. It is also about the absence of positive ones. When you feel engaged with your job, your work is enriched by your excitement about its challenges, satisfaction in a job well done, enjoyment of your relationships with others, and pride in enacting your values. These positive emotions foster commitment and motivation—if the work makes you feel good, you'll want to keep doing it and doing it well. In addition, when you're feeling good, you're willing to put in extra effort, do something special. You're creative and open to new solutions. The enjoyment of successes can balance out the pain of failures, whether the successes are big achievements or small everyday expressions of appreciation from others. But when positive feelings erode to the point that they no longer have the power to offset the negatives, cynicism looms large. Everything is judged and experienced negatively with distrust and hostility. The half-full glass is *always* half-empty.

The Social Context of Emotions

George had worked for a telephone company ever since graduating from high school and had gradually moved up to an important sales job. He took a great deal of pride in his work and usually placed among the top five in sales each year. He was also very proud of his affiliation with the company that was, he said, "One of the good guys in the community." In fact, he often volunteered time and effort for the charitable events the company sponsored. But recently the company went through a major downsizing, and George was laid off. As such a loyal and dedicated employee, he was shocked and stunned by this "involuntary severance."

Six months later, George was asked to return to the company—this time as a contract worker on the payroll of a temporary employment agency. In other words, George would be rented back to the company that had fired him. Although his hourly wage would be higher, he would have no benefits, no seniority, and no chance of future promotion. George eventually took the job because he needed the income, but his bitterness was evident. "I feel as if I've been lied to and betrayed. They told me they didn't need the work I did, but obviously they do. But they want it cheap. They don't want to give me what I'm worth. And they clearly don't give a damn about everything else I've done for them over the years. So the hell with them—if they don't care about me, I'm not going to care about the job I do. The 'good guys.' What a joke."

Although George is working for the company again, he no longer attempts to be tops in sales and no longer goes the extra mile to get the job done. He spends the minimum amount of time at the office and isolates himself from the other employees. When customers complain, he no longer leaps to the company's defense; indeed, sometimes he even joins in the bad-mouthing. His anger has clearly eroded the quality of his work.

Emotion does not simply mark the transformation from engagement to burnout, it also mediates it. The emotional highs we experience as enjoyment, satisfaction, and pride are critical in driving important work behaviors. These feelings motivate us to do our work well, to seek ways to improve, to cooperate with colleagues, to be committed to the job. In contrast, the emotional lows of anger or anxiety are detrimental to the quality of job performance.

When people express the negative emotions of burnout, social relationships can be devastated. Normal conversations become charged with hostility and irritation, turning everyday social encounters into unpleasant occasions. Rudeness, sarcasm, criticism, and insults become the rule rather than the exception. Disagreements between colleagues or between workers and management escalate into pitched battles. Collaborative teamwork disintegrates. The quality of customer service goes downhill too. Even relationships with family and friends are not spared this emotional negativity.

This is how burnout begins its downward spiral. As these negative emotions get expressed, they generate negative and dysfunctional responses. Of course, hostility breeds more hostility—snap at people, and people are likely to snap back. In this sense, burnout is contagious. But hostility also leads others to withdraw—people don't want to be around you anymore. You may not consider this an undesirable outcome when you feel sick and tired of people, and this is why detachment and distancing are typical with burnout. But this self-imposed social isolation has its costs too, because it erodes your ability to get the emotional nurturing that comes from the love and support of your friends and family.

Basically, emotions are not just private and personal but rather *social* experiences, both in their origin and their effect. When we express our negative feelings it affects the world around us, making it a more unpleasant place, and this in turn fuels our negative feelings—and the downward spiral continues. The same spiral process, but in a positive upward direction, occurs when we are engaged with our work—our positive feelings encourage positive responses from others and our world becomes ever better, producing more positive feelings in us.

Given the important role of emotions in work motivation, job performance, and collegial relationships, they are surprisingly underrated by most people. Why is this so? To some extent, it's because jobs are defined in terms of skills and outcomes. Within this framework, feelings are seen to be subsidiary. Feelings are considered to be personal; the individual bears full responsibility for them. Feelings are often viewed as irrelevant to the job task ("It doesn't matter if you love it or hate it—you just have to *do* it"). Sometimes feelings are seen as distinct liabilities that can interfere with the job. For example, health care workers need to hide from their patients any feelings of disgust or sorrow, and service personnel need to hide their boredom or irritation under an ever-present cheeriness. In these instances, it is up to the individual to manage his or her emotions and bring them under control. Unfortunately, when we view emotion as a function of the individual alone we ignore how much it is also a function of the social context.

Emotions arise from our contact with the world around us and shape our responses to it. An event occurs, and our judgments about that event and its meaning to us sparks a particular emotional response. In other words, emotions are the means for translating *outside* events into *personal* terms. Our emotions, in turn, often guide our reaction to the event. For example, suppose a co-worker has criticized you for making some mistakes that she had to correct. You might feel guilty about messing up the job and letting her down, and normally, because you feel guilty, you would be sure to do the job more carefully next time or offer to do something extra to make it up to her. But if you judge her criticism to be unfair, you might feel angry about her remarks, and that anger might lead you to make some hostile remarks in return or refuse any future requests she may make of you.

Emotions play an important role in our sense of right and wrong. It is not the logic of our moral beliefs but the intensity of our feelings that propels us to take action against injustice. If we are morally outraged by some inequity, then we want to do something to put things right. Injustice usually involves a mismatch between the way things are and the way they should be. So it should come as no surprise that the six mismatches in job-person fit provoke strong emotions about injustice in the workplace. These strong emotions can lead to strong actions, some of which are not particularly moral themselves (for example, an employee who feels angry about being treated unfairly justifies stealing company supplies by thinking that "they owe it to me"). The point is, emotion is a key to understanding how burnout arises from the lack of fit between worker and workplace.

A FAILURE TO FIT IN

Because burnout is so visible in the emotions and behaviors of individual employees, the common wisdom is that it is a "people problem" rather than a job problem.

According to one common view, people who experience burnout are weak. They lack the physical constitution or the psychological resilience necessary to manage the demands of work. The work world is a tough arena in which only the fit survive; burnout is a failure to survive.

Another view is that people who experience burnout are unreasonable. Some people complain about everything; burnout is just another way of complaining.

To others, burnout is a psychiatric disorder. Burnout is simply what clinical depression looks like when the patient manages to make it to work.

Or burnout is a symptom of problems at home. Difficulties with a marriage or with children wear a person down, reducing the capacity to work effectively.

Blaming the Person

A popular but erroneous perception is behind all these opinions: burnout is the person's fault. The logic suggests that people bring this problem on themselves and so have sole responsibility for fixing it. Perhaps this view is so popular because people describe their experiences of burnout in personal terms and tend to look for personal solutions—going to counseling or making midlife career changes, for example. Furthermore, when people feel distant and isolated, it reconfirms their idea that burnout is a symptom of their personal shortcomings or failures. Psychiatrists, clinical psychologists, and social workers support this perspective, viewing burnout as a psychiatric disorder that is amenable to individual treatment approaches.

The extent to which people buy into the individual perspective on burnout often depends on whether they are experiencing it themselves or observing it in someone else. The insider's view of burnout is not the same as an outsider's. For example, imagine what a supervisor might say about an employee who is burned out, compared with the employee's version. The supervisor sees a drop in productivity, and assumes it is due to laziness, lack of motivation, or incompetence. The employee, however, sees not only the decline in work but also the emotional turmoil, the conflicts, and the demands that preceded it; thus, the employee is more likely to attribute it to frustrating circumstances and work overload. That difference in perspective can lead to misinterpretations, miscommunications, and more conflict.

Insiders may also conceal their feelings from the outside world, and this widens the gap between the two perspectives. People often keep their feelings private. Sometimes they worry that their feelings are inappropriate or unprofessional, as when they have strong feelings toward a client. Or they may be embarrassed by their reactions and worried about what others might think of them, as when a manager loses a public showdown with an irate customer. Thus, the image that people project to the outside world does not always match their internal state. They may appear calm and collected even when they are worried and upset, or they may appear unfeeling and impersonal even when they are concerned and caring. Because of this discrepancy, people can easily be misjudged by the outside world.

As far as the organization is concerned, when burnout is seen to be a personal experience—the result of problematic behavior and poor productivity—it becomes a personnel problem rather than a strategic management problem. When burnout is seen to be an individual problem, it can be handled through established organizational support systems that focus on individual employees, such as employee assistance programs or stress training. When the process is seen as being under the individual's control, people are made accountable for their own level of burnout.

We agree that people experience burnout as a personal problem and that they have a part to play in preventing or alleviating it, but we do not agree that people are totally responsible for its occurrence or solution. Why do we think the individual viewpoint is wrong? Its fundamental flaw is that it looks only at the person and ignores the context. Our research and consulting work provide clear and consistent evidence that the roots of burnout stretch far beyond the individual into the work environment. Burnout does not result from a genetic predisposition to grumpiness, a depressive personality, or general weakness. It is not caused by a failure of character or a lack of ambition. It is not a personality defect or a clinical syndrome. It is an occupational problem.

Understanding the Situation

Considering the current crisis in the workplace, it is not surprising to find people in personal crisis. As we discussed in Chapter One, disruptive changes in the nature of work are occurring because of global competition, technological innovation, tighter control systems, and unjust compensation. As a result, organizations are strained, forced to increase productivity, redesign operations, and survive the opportunistic exploitation of people trying to get rich fast. The stresses and strains of major social changes have to end up somewhere. Most of the time, they end up in the minds and bodies of people. People absorb them and turn them into physical and psychological stress. We do not mean this in an esoteric sense. We are not talking about the fine points of chaos theory, which suggests that the flutter of a butterfly's wing in one place somehow causes hurricanes on the other side of the globe. We are talking about something much more straightforward and commonplace.

Organizations are complex systems comprising many interacting components of varying size and quality. They adjust to strains imposed on them by rearranging the size and interrelationships of these components. These interventions upset the relationships with work that individuals have established within these components. They are now in disarray. So after the organization as a whole has resolved its problem, the component parts still have to make adjustments.

Let's say an organization addresses its financial strains by cutting the operating budgets of its departments. Now the organization has a balanced budget but the departments have the strain of a budget shortfall. When a department reacts to its budget problem, it passes the strain along to its component parts—the people who work in it. The first people to get hit with the strain are the managers, because they have to deal with cuts to their staffing or operating budgets that are beyond their control. Through their best efforts, managers may lessen the damage but they cannot insulate their employees completely from the consequences.

Julie and her fellow teachers are clear examples of how individual employees become the "shock absorbers" for organizational strains. To deal with its financial problems, the school district cut the budgets for each of its schools. At Julie's school, the principal had to figure out how to teach all the necessary classes with less money. Some clerical and janitorial staff positions were reduced to part-time, class size was increased, some art and music classes were eliminated, cutbacks were made in classroom supplies and photocopying, and extracurricular activities were reduced. All the teachers retained their jobs, but with no cost-of-living salary increases.

Julie found that she was teaching more students in larger classes and consequently had less time to give individual attention to each child. She could no longer get all the teaching materials she needed unless she paid for some of them out of her own pocket. She had to do clerical work and housekeeping chores in addition to teaching. She was asked to volunteer to cover more afterschool activities so that they could be continued for the students. Meanwhile, the school as a whole became a dirtier and less pleasant place to be.

Thus, downsizing initiates a process in which the larger organization resolves its problems by reducing resources available to departments, and departments pass the problems down the line to individuals. They balance their reduced budgets by reducing their staffs. Part of the resulting strain goes to the clientele, who have to wait in longer lines or lose services entirely. A bigger part of the burden goes to the employees, especially the ones who lose their jobs. They now have to relocate, retrain, and adjust their personal finances.

But the people who hold onto their jobs feel the strain as well. They worry about the security of their jobs. They feel the pressure to work harder, to process cases more quickly, to work longer hours. It is important to keep the work group productive, and to be seen as a major contributor to its efforts. Nobody wants to be a prime candidate for the next round of cuts, particularly if there are few opportunities for other employment. In a stagnant economy, when downsizing has reduced employment opportunities, people are more likely to continue in work relationships that do not meet their expectations in order to survive.

A Cascade Effect

People working on the front lines also experience the strain of addressing complaints from disgruntled clients. Service reductions and cost increases do not go over well in the best of times, and they are even less welcome when times are bad. The result is hassles and conflict. Front-line staff often lack the resources, time, and energy necessary to establish a mutually acceptable working relationship with clients so the conflict persists, adding to the demands of the job.

Cindy is a home care nurse with a Canadian public agency responsible for seniors. Her caseload increased significantly when the hospitals in the region addressed their budgetary pressures by reducing the number of days patients remain in the hospital following treatment. Cindy's agency ended up with the extended care that could not be handled by the patients' families. The hospital eased its financial strain by passing the cost of caring for some of its patients to the home care agency. But although the agency now had the strain of additional cases, it was unsuccessful in obtaining additional funding from a government determined to reduce health care costs. The agency addressed the strain of additional clients by increasing the standard caseloads of the nurses. So Cindy and the other nurses visited cases less frequently, shortened the visits they made, and did less for the clients.

Now Cindy cannot provide what she considers to be adequate care, but she does not want to desert her job and her clients. However, the clients' anger at the drop in services has been directed at Cindy and the other nurses rather than at the agency or the hospital or the government. Thus, a strain that began at the broad economic and political level has worked its way down to the personal relationship between patient and nurse. Cindy feels trapped in a bad situation: she has clear values about the quality of patient care but lacks the means to put those values into practice. This strain affects her relationship with her work and increases her vulnerability to burnout.

Thus, strain cascades down from the broad political and economic arena, through regional policy, to a local organization and, finally, to individuals. The actions taken to solve problems at one level become the source of problems at the next level down. In this way, a realignment of global economic patterns leads to strains down the line. Where these strains end up is with the front-line employees whose options for adjustment are limited—and who thus are at greater risk for burnout.

The moral of the story is that although it is the person who experiences burnout, it is the job situation that is the primary cause. Specifically, a mismatch between the person and the job causes burnout, and right now, because of the current crisis in the workplace, the match between people and jobs is highly strained. As we have seen, the six mismatches between person and job are the key sources of burnout, so let's look at them more closely in Chapter Three.

3

What Causes Burnout?

Now that we have seen what it feels like to experience burnout, our next task is to identify what causes it. As we have also seen, the causes lie more in the job environment than in the individual. But more specifically, the causes can be traced to the six mismatches between people and their jobs that we described in Chapter One: work overload, lack of control, insufficient reward, breakdown in community, absence of fairness, and conflicting values. The more we study burnout, the more we talk with concerned managers, and the more we interview employees in crisis, the more clearly we see the impact of these six mismatches on people's well-being. So let's try to get a deeper understanding of just what is happening in these six areas.

WORK OVERLOAD

Workload is a key dimension of organizational life. From the organization's perspective, workload means productivity. From the individual's perspective, workload means time and energy. Finding a compromise between the two perspectives is a fundamental challenge in maintaining a balanced relationship with work. Major organizational transitions associated with downsizing and restructuring target workload first and foremost. In their scramble for increased productivity, organizations push people beyond what they can sustain.

Workload includes how much you do and what you do. The current crisis in the workplace affects the workload in three ways: it is more intense, it demands more time, and it is more complex. Not surprisingly, relief is hard to find.

Work Is More Intense

The point of downsizing and other strategies for increasing productivity is for fewer people to do more work. Teachers are dealing with larger enrollments, nurses are responsible for more patients, and bank tellers are handling more transactions. Ideally, by working smarter—not working harder—people can do more with less. Through better design, smoother work flow, and reduced busywork, organizations can enable a smaller workforce to become more productive. But this goal is rarely attained. Increased productivity is more often achieved because employees work harder for longer hours than because management is smarter. The organizations' increased productivity comes at the cost of staff members' greater effort. But it is important to remember that this kind of effort is a temporary quality of human performance.

It is hard to find relief at work. Restful moments between events are gone. Each demand rolls without a break into the next. There is no time to catch your breath. Organizations seem to be testing the theory that people can work flat-out forever. But, with no time to recover, people soon find that their exhaustion just builds. Additional demands might be manageable if they were given more resources; extra support or equipment can turn increased demand into an opportunity. But instead, the current scramble for survival often results in a shortage of resources.

It is also hard to find relief outside of work. People are busier in every domain of their lives: children, aging parents, houses, and other responsibilities fill much of the day. There is less money to smooth the way. Through the late 1970s and 1980s, families dealt with financial pressures by working more. Of course, a lot of that extra income was eaten up by the costs of running a two-income household: child care, second car, clothing, and travel. In the 1990s, even the illusion of increasing income is unattainable for most people. With both members of a couple already working, there is no one else to send into the fray; meanwhile, family income levels are decreasing. Less money translates into working harder at home to keep things going smoothly. There are fewer vacations and more worries. People do not recover when they return home from work; the demands continue.

> Linda is a vice president at a large company. The board of directors recently announced a merger with another company and appointed a new CEO. Linda's day has abruptly been filled with an endless list of meetings at the two companies to manage the transition. Meanwhile, the company continues to provide services. All of Linda's prior responsibilities remain while she takes on this major task. So she squeezes more contacts with more people into a workday that is only so big. She stretches the limits with early morning meetings and evenings in the office. But there remains the matter of getting her daughters to school, driving them to swim team practices, and helping with the math homework.
>
> One Saturday she drives to the office, passing a poster that reads, "From the Labor Movement: The People Who Brought You the Weekend," and wonders for a moment whether having a management position is all that it is cracked up to be. She just tries to move faster, going from one intense meeting to the next. The staff are worried about the future of their jobs. And Linda herself knows that once the transition is complete, she will have to compete for her position with her counterpart at the other company.

Work Demands More Time

The lengthening workweek is exhausting. For decades, unions successfully negotiated shorter workweeks, but those gains are slipping away. People in professional and front-line management positions are working longer hours but are still not able to keep up with overwhelming demands. They arrive for breakfast meetings—where more often than not they supply their own bagels—munch sandwiches at their computer keyboards, and work into the evening. They work on their computers at home to prepare for the next day. More work gets done, but at a cost. Such long, intense workdays deplete energy. Individuals give up personal time and commitments to help the organization appear more productive. But the productivity gains are illusory and temporary.

Work Is More Complex

Jobs are becoming increasingly complex as people are "multitasking"—taking on more roles simultaneously. For example, it used to be enough for a cashier at a university cafeteria to collect money from customers, but now the job involves making coffee, cleaning the area, and keeping inventory. Because a primary target of downsizing interventions has been middle management, the work of former middle managers has been distributed across the organization, giving everyone more forms to complete, more calls to return, more meetings to attend. This trend is especially evident in the public service sector. Teachers, nurses, professors, and police officers are finding more of their time consumed by administrative drudgery.

Work Creates the Exhaustion of Overload

Exhaustion—emotional, creative, or physical—undermines effectiveness, health, and well-being. When we talk with people about exhaustion, we see that they are clearly frustrated with their inability to accomplish what is truly important to them. It takes energy just to make it through the day. It takes considerably more energy to work in a creative, focused manner, solve complicated problems, and keep people fully informed of your contributions to collaborative projects. It takes energy to focus on others with genuine attention and respect; exhaustion undermines the capacity to work with feeling. The breakdown in the relationship with work increases these demands because individuals are attending more closely to their employment situation, not just to their jobs. Because you can take nothing for granted, you have to spend more of your precious energy anticipating organizational problems. Positioning yourself to deal with downsizing and job restructuring is exhausting.

People experiencing the exhaustion of burnout describe chronic problems with their health: sleeplessness, tension, headaches, high blood pressure, ulcers, and greater susceptibility to colds and flus. It is impossible to feel truly relaxed or comfortable. Health problems perpetuate exhaustion if you continue working despite feeling miserable. Yet although work may be wearing you out, you cannot stay away, because you have a sense of duty and obligation to co-workers, or because you are afraid you will be replaced. As we noted in Chapter Two, energy is a fundamental quality of engagement. Unless you have a viable and enduring way to maintain your energy, you cannot maintain balanced relationships with work. To avoid exhaustion, you must be able to exercise control over critical aspects of your work.

LACK OF CONTROL

The capacity to set priorities for day-to-day work, select approaches to doing work, and make decisions about the use of resources is central to being a professional. Policies that interfere with this capacity reduce individual autonomy and involvement with work. When people do not have control over important dimensions of their job, it prevents them from addressing problems that they identify. The issue is not whether they are able or willing to take action but rather whether the organization will tolerate creative problem solving outside of its centralized control structures. Without the capacity to make relevant decisions, people can waste time doing things that do not get the job done. Without control, they cannot balance their interests with those of the organization. They lose interest if they do not feel that they are making things happen.

James is a bank manager who is attempting to put together an early retirement fund before he burns out completely. Although he feels secure in his position, he is constantly frustrated by what he perceives as a lack of control over important aspects of his job. The rules and policies will not let him do the job in a way that makes sense. He does not have control over the resources he needs to initiate new programs. His supervisor second-guesses his decisions, taking away what little control James had managed to create for himself. On a larger level, central management takes away control by making up policies that are completely at odds with the way things actually work in the bank. Human resource management is bogged down with union rules and government regulations. James cannot imagine having enough control to identify an opportunity in his work, gather resources, and implement a strategy. The control systems of the organization are killing his initiative. At one time the organization at least provided security in exchange, but that meager compensation is gone. Now, it just interferes.

How Much Control?

Control is a relative thing. No one has complete control in an organization. CEOs are lucky if they manage to identify the small percentage of an organization they actually control, and CEOs have more control than most people. Why is it so difficult to exercise control at work?

First, almost everything you do in an organization involves collaborating with other people, all of whom want to exercise control over their work. Thus, organizational control is shared. One person's autonomy stops where another person's begins. Second, most interesting work involves dealing with the unpredictable. An important part of the challenge of developing a new product is dealing with the unexpected problems that arise along the way. If project management were completely predictable and controllable, it would not be challenging. Unilateral control over every aspect of your work is not a reasonable goal. It is not even desirable: absolute control has never been noted for contributing to a charming personality. But there is a limit to how little control people can have and still maintain a productive relationship with work. If they have no control over important aspects of the job—whether that control is individual or shared—people are vulnerable to the exhaustion, cynicism, and ineffectiveness of burnout.

The Burden of Micromanagement

Micromanagement is the opposite of bottom-line management. Instead of allowing staff members to act with accountability for the bottom line, a micromanaged organization centralizes control through detailed policies. It limits the range of approaches staff members can use to address a problem, and it reviews decisions prior to implementation.

Staff members generally interpret micromanagement as a lack of trust because such policies deny them the opportunity to use their professional judgment. Indeed it may be that central management does not trust staff, but this is not necessarily the case. Instead, management may be intensely concerned with cost controls, hope to change central values in the organizational culture, or be under pressure to show short-term results. Characterizing a particular management style as micromanagement is something of a judgment call. Those seen to be micromanaging generally put a positive spin on their efforts: they insist that it is a matter of instituting necessary organizational controls or providing guidance.

An alternative to micromanagement is an effective rewards system. Organizations can ensure active cooperation among the staff if they communicate their values and encourage certain activities by recognizing and rewarding staff members' contributions.

INSUFFICIENT REWARD

The current crisis in the work environment reduces the capacity of organizations to reward people in meaningful ways. People hope that their jobs will bring them the material rewards of money, prestige, and security, but lately jobs have been bringing less of all three even as people are working more. An even greater contributor to the experience of burnout is the loss of the intrinsic reward of doing enjoyable work—and building expertise—with respected colleagues. The combined loss of extrinsic and intrinsic rewards diminishes the potential for work to be engaging.

Getting Less for More

Money is tight, especially in organizations that are undergoing major restructuring. Companies ask employees to take pay cuts in order to stay viable in the face of competition. Their ability to move jobs to developing nations at greatly reduced salaries provides effective leverage in wage negotiations. In addition to cutting pay, organizations have reduced their fringe benefit costs. They define a larger percentage of jobs as part-time or contract work in order to avoid providing benefits altogether. When they do provide benefits, they cut the biggest cost item—health insurance—through the use of managed care. These plans can provide excellent services but are themselves under constant pressure to reduce costs. Furthermore, often what appears to be a cost reduction is actually just a shift in responsibility from the employer to the individual. For example, these insurance plans may cost the employer less, but they entail ongoing costs for the individuals using them. The corporate saving is balanced against an individual cost. Together, such constraints disrupt the balance of rewards and contributions between staff members and their organizations.

Public sector employees throughout North America have faced wage freezes and rollbacks. Governments have passed legislation to suspend collective agreements in order to get their budget expenditures under control. They have rolled back salaries, frozen scheduled pay increments, and used back-to-work legislation to counter public sector strikes. Job reductions throughout the public sector eliminate for many the possibility of finding a better-paying job elsewhere. Increased workloads exacerbate the impact of reduced compensation, yet people are stuck in unrewarding jobs. Instead of steady financial growth throughout their careers, people in both the public and private sectors are encountering financial stagnation or losses.

Even when salaries remain steady, purchasing power decreases through a proliferation of direct and indirect taxes. Since 1983 social security tax increases have been particularly steep as the United States and Canada have acknowledged that their government pension systems were inadequately funded to meet the demands of an aging population. Throughout the late 1980s and early 1990s excise taxes on alcohol, tobacco, and gasoline were increased to generate more revenue. The ethic of user pay has turned into a significant source of revenue for government agencies. A wide array of agencies have introduced fees for services that were previously free: application forms, national park campsites, art gallery admissions. Universities and hospitals are increasing fees sharply in response to reduced subsidies from national, state, and local governments. An irritating nuisance tax introduced in 1990 in the United States is an annual Coast Guard fee on recreational boats, which ranges from $25 to $100. Our Canadian counterparts did not have the audacity to add this fee until 1996. In the United States, the Clinton administration rejected the regressive taxation of the Bush and Reagan eras, while in Canada the liberal Chretien government rejected the similar Mulroney government. But they continued most of these fees. You see, they needed the money. The broad impact of these new taxes and fees is to reduce a salary's buying power. At the same time, middle-income taxpayers are more at risk for tax audits as Internal Revenue offices more closely scrutinize middle-class tax breaks, such as those for child care and home offices. Working people end up with a reduced standard of living despite working harder in a more stressful, uncertain environment.

At the same time, the likelihood of a second material reward of work has diminished as well: there are fewer opportunities for career advancement. Just as administrative positions start to look good to maturing baby boomers, thinning organizational structures have resulted in fewer positions to which people may be promoted.

Indeed, flattened organizational structures often mean management chores without the perks; as middle management positions disappear, many of their administrative tasks are delegated to the ranks. So people accomplish these tasks without the reward of a prestigious position in the organization.

A third material reward that is being lost is job security. Instead of recognizing years of loyal contributions with an assured position of trust, organizations are reducing their commitment to long-term staff. Job security is a reward in itself, as well as a means through which other rewards occur. For example, salary scales are structured so that people move from low pay at the beginning of a career to higher pay as they gain seniority and are promoted. That is the career profile: the high salary at the end compensates for the low pay at the beginning. But when careers are terminated partway because of downsizing, dismissal, or forced early retirement, the overall compensation package is greatly reduced. Salary scales that span an entire career are lost along with job security.

Losing the Joy of Work

A more profound reward problem is the loss of intrinsic satisfaction. People who are good at what they do enjoy the process of the work itself. The process of doing the work sets up a pleasant concentration of attention and energy that creates a kind of flow. They respond to a complex situation such as a client's problem, a diagnostic question, or a technical puzzle by bringing their skills and experience to bear with creative initiative. This is what the job is all about. Attaining that state of mind as an individual or in a team is work's most effective reward. The point of management is ultimately to bring about conditions that permit that sort of work to happen while pursuing the organization's mission.

Changes in the nature of work are getting in the way of that experience. Work overload prevents people from attending to it thoroughly. Centralized control undermines their capacity to approach the work in the most effective manner. The same dynamics and pressures break up work teams: understaffed groups with constantly changing staff members cannot establish that kind of flow in their work.

As a result, the workplace has been polarized. Dedicated professionals see themselves as doing good work in spite of management rather than with its assistance. At one time, professionals saw management as an important source of support as they worked to address the demands of clients. Job security and professional development in both the public and private sectors helped them feel that their jobs were manageable and enjoyable. Now, with that support diminishing, front-line service professionals are often at odds with management. They find themselves agreeing with clients that crucial services are being discontinued as part of management strategies to contain costs. Management has become more often a source of problems than of solutions. This is not a sustainable way of running organizations. This kind of environment also contributes to the exhaustion, cynicism, and lack of effectiveness that characterize burnout.

The lack of rewards is not simply a consequence of tight money. However, a scarcity of money increases the importance that people put on rewards when they evaluate their work, causing both staff members and the organization as a whole to take a more materialistic view. This is the wrong focus. Productive people in high-performance organizations focus on the work, not on its potential for material gain. The long-term potential of a company, its capacity to convey genuine concern for its clientele, and its commitment to an ethical approach to business are hurt when there is a preoccupation with financial gain at the personal or the corporate level. Finally, as work becomes more strained, less enjoyable, and less rewarding, people have less quality time with co-workers, and where they work becomes less of a community.

BREAKDOWN OF COMMUNITY

The fourth impact of the current crisis is the breakdown of community at work. Community is undermined through the loss of job security and an excessive focus on short-term profit that excludes consideration of people. On one level, this atmosphere fragments the personal relationships that are the fundamental components of community in an organization. On a second level, it undermines the teamwork that is seen to be increasingly central to the manufacturing, information processing, and service sectors of the economy. The loss of community is evident in greater conflict among people, less mutual support and respect, and a growing sense of isolation. A sense of belonging disappears when people work separately instead of together.

Fragmenting Personal Relationships

Life in an organization comes down to contacts with people. The day-to-day interactions within your immediate work group are the elements of your personal experience of an organization. Regardless of how rigid, stuffy, or predictable a job may seem, your contacts with other people are unique: nobody else discusses the same issues with the same people or has the same feelings as you do. If nothing else, you are the only person in your group who does not talk to you. Furthermore, your social world at work is ongoing, and it influences your thoughts and feelings. In the course of talking with others about work, personal issues, or world events, you build a shared idea of these occurrences. Personal relationships at work become an integral part of who you are.

When there is no job security, the close personal links that are the basic elements of community are fragmented. As organizations weaken their commitment to their people, staff members have less of a basis for making commitments to one another. They become reluctant to get seriously involved in the lives of people who may well be making a brief sojourn through the organization with little opportunity to become a part of the community. Shorter-term contracts address only a part of a person. The organization calls upon an individual's skills and energy without making a commitment to developing that person's potential over the long run. This approach to staffing encourages a utilitarian view of people that impoverishes the social environment of the organization.

Bob and Vivian had nothing to say to each other while packing to leave Massachusetts. They had gotten their hopes up that things would work out this time. They had been so sure that this move would be their last for a long time. They had been wrong. The new move they were packing for was their fourth in six years. They made each move hoping that it would take them to the place where they would settle. That hope was getting more strained with time.

It was pretty clear that no one at the Massachusetts branch of the large telecommunications company had believed that Bob and Vivian would be around for long, and they were proved right. They had seen enough people move in and out of the switch assembly operation as major orders came and went. Everyone had been polite, but they had kept their distance. Bob and Vivian had never even begun to make any lasting friendships.

The children took it really hard. Now Bob did not even try to convince them that the move to the Ohio branch plant would be the last. He and Vivian both felt really tired. It seemed impossible to make an impact on the most important decisions affecting their lives. It would be a lot easier if they just did not care anymore.

Undermining Teamwork

A utilitarian attitude toward individual employees extends to work groups as well. Shorter-term contracts reduce the potential for groups to develop a smooth and unique flow to their work together. Frequent mergers and acquisitions break up teams as organizations reassign people across the newly constructed entity. Often, team members must compete to retain their positions against their counterparts in the newly formed company. Those who are successful must build a sense of teamwork with a new group of people, all of whom are uncertain about the team's potential to survive in the long run.

Jill couldn't believe that she did not have a supervisor. All the talk about the new workplace had been well and good. Everyone had felt relieved when, during the last budget crunch, the employment center where she worked as a counselor decided to take out the supervisor positions, leaving the people in each office to manage themselves as groups. But it did not work. The group's sense of community over the past six months had declined. Five of the eleven people in the so-called team had been replaced as the result of transfers and early retirement, and the new people were on temporary contracts. There was no shared sense within this group. To make matters worse, the company's goals had changed so much over the past year that the group found it impossible to operate effectively. They could not figure out what anyone else really expected of them and they could not define their own values as a group. It is hard to be self-directing when you do not know what direction you want to take. Jill just felt nervous. She spent most of her time trying to avoid making any mistakes that might get her into trouble.

Working Separately, Not Together

Without community, a group of people lack the synergy of an integrated work group. They are simply a bunch of individuals, more likely to get in one another's way than to enhance their performance as a group. Furthermore, a lack of community is not merely a problem for the workers. A lack of community constitutes a major loss for the organization, which receives much less back in productivity.

Organizations that lack community are vulnerable to conflict among their members. When people perceive that co-workers are failing to carry their weight, they often become angry or bitter. If people do not have a strong commitment to working together, such conflicts tend to linger on. Although active debate and effective conflict resolution can build a sense of community in an otherwise dull group, unresolved conflict tends to bog people down and ultimately hurts an organization's capacity to function. Unresolved conflict is an emotional drain on the energy people need for creative tasks. Warring factions within a work group can bring it to a standstill. A work group in conflict works against itself. The conflict may be between objectives or between strategies for attaining objectives. In either case, people will waste energy and time working at odds with one another.

Community is cost-effective. Conflict takes time. Debating issues, gossiping about the problem, mulling over the conflict—all divert time and energy from work. The impact of conflict on a work group is to deplete the energy available for effective work. Pervasive conflict also sets the stage for the fifth major problem in current organizations: a lack of fairness.

ABSENCE OF FAIRNESS

A workplace is perceived to be fair when three key elements are present: trust, openness, and respect. When an organization achieves community, people trust one another to fulfill their roles in shared projects, to communicate openly about their intentions, and to show mutual respect. When an organization acts fairly, it values every person who contributes to its success, it indicates that every individual is important. All three elements of fairness are essential to maintaining a person's engagement with work. In contrast, their absence contributes directly to burnout.

In the current crisis, organizations are hard-pressed to maintain communities of trust, openness, and mutual respect. First, as they scramble for survival, they take actions that indicate relatively little concern for their employees' welfare. They devote their resources to short-term financial performance rather than to the less clear-cut goal of building organizational community. Employees do not trust management to make decisions that are in the best interests of the clients, the employees, or the organization itself. Management does not take staff members' assessment of service priorities at face value. Instead, staff members are perceived as being primarily concerned with protecting their occupational role or their professional prerogatives, and only secondarily concerned with the welfare of clients. Discussions between management and staff can become bogged down in mutual distrust.

Second, the current crisis diminishes open and honest communication in organizations. Competitive pressure and short-term management values encourage secrecy. Central management is often slow to release information about its plans. Sometimes management itself does not know what will happen very far into the future; a turbulent environment makes planning difficult if not irrelevant. When organizations cannot anticipate their revenues or major expenses, they cannot stick to detailed strategic plans. When they do develop plans, they are reluctant to communicate the information because it may give their competitors an advantage. Knowledge of their plans may also have an adverse impact on their own staff. For example, announcing a major restructuring will certainly cause anxiety among many staff members and may prompt valued people to leave in pursuit of career opportunities while the organization still needs them. It is hard to find organizations that are open and honest communicators; often when they are found they are not trusted. Cynical distrust breeds more cynicism.

As one social worker put it, "I never get the sense that I am being told the truth about the things going on around here. And why not? I have to implement all these policy changes, so why not let me know the reasons for them? I'm an intelligent adult after all—I think I can handle it."

In the current crisis, organizations often also take actions that hurt the third element of fairness, respect for people. An exclusive focus on the bottom line necessarily encourages a manipulative view of people because they are valued only to the extent that they fit into the corporate plan. For many employees, the manner in which organizations carry out downsizing and restructuring offers a glaring example of unfairness. Organizations make decisions about what and who to cut according to opportunism or at best a corporate plan that is removed from the organization's day-to-day life. As a result, creative employees, especially people recently hired, lose their jobs while less productive workers in other sectors of the organization remain. The problem becomes evident when organizations find it necessary to hire back on contract the very employees they laid off in order to address problems that exceed the grasp of the employees they retained.

Despite a proliferation of formal mechanisms for ensuring fairness and respect, many people are losing confidence in the willingness or ability of organizations to operate in this manner. The extravagant compensation packages given to CEOs, which we discussed in Chapter One, provide a reference point against which people evaluate fairness. Such uneven and unfair distribution of rewards destroys a sense of community and undermines productive relationships with work.

Jane was a science professor in a research university. A new laboratory facility was being built on campus, and all the professors had been polled about how much lab space they needed, what configuration they preferred, and so on. The basic operating principle was that the lab space would be divided fairly among the faculty according to their individual needs—depending on their research interests, some professors needed more space than others. However, just prior to the move into the new lab, Jane discovered that she was getting less space than she had requested—far less, in fact, than her current laboratory had. According to the dean, it was just one of the unfortunate effects of budget reductions—everyone would have to make do with less. But on further checking, Jane found out that she was the only professor who was having to make do—in fact, a newly hired professor was being given a huge laboratory, including some of the space that had been originally assigned to her.

When Jane confronted the dean about this, he told her that he had had to make a special deal with the new professor, in order to make the hire, and that he had assumed that Jane, being such a nice person, would not be as upset as some of the other professors might have been about losing lab space. Quite the contrary, Jane was furious about the unfairness of it all. Her expectation of fair treatment had been violated, she had not been treated with the same respect as the other professors, and she had been lied to by her superiors.

Underlying concerns for trust, openness, and respect is the question of values. The community of an organization is built upon shared values. When values are in conflict, there is no basis of agreement on which to build a sense of community.

CONFLICTING VALUES

Values influence everything about your relationship with work. The current crisis in the job environment is in many ways a major value conflict. A short-term survival-and-profit value system is going against values that the most dedicated employees hold about their work. What people find especially aggravating is that often organizations emphasize a dedication to excellent service or production while they take actions that damage the quality of work. In fact, management is not attempting to undermine quality, it is just attending to other things. Excellent quality requires total attention.

What Is Really Important?

Organizations that make much of their commitment to customer service are removing the personal quality of their relationships with customers. For example, over the past decade banks have pushed customers out of the main lobby into the foyer with automatic teller machines. They are currently pushing them entirely out of the building with dial-in banking. Another example is the near-impossibility of finding a person on the other end of the phone line at major airlines or retailers. The range of personalized options that can be provided by a trained professional are replaced with a fixed-choice menu buried somewhere in a voice mail script. Access and cheap service have taken the place of personal contact.

The primary values guiding customer service are to be efficient, accurate, personal, and adapted to individuals. Excellent customer service combines features of all four. But you often have to make trade-offs among these four qualities: sometimes services are less accurate in order to be completed on time. Adapting services to the needs of a specific customer may require bending rules or creating features that are not part of the standard options. Banking machines trade the personal touch for greater accessibility.

Different services suit different clients. For example, Karl has never used an ATM machine because he enjoys chatting with the teller when banking and, now that he is retired, he can organize his life to accommodate a visit to the bank during regular hours. The greater accessibility offered by the ATM is of no value to him compared with the greater personal quality of interactions with a teller. But another customer is grateful for the greater efficiency of accessible ATM machines. A large bank can provide a range of services to suit the varied values of a diverse clientele; a small business has to make hard choices in offering its more limited range of services. Any organization at any time has to choose among the values it will emphasize in its services.

The current crisis forces organizations to make choices that are inconsistent with their core values and those of its staff members. Concern for short-term financial performance can result in organizations neglecting the more costly aspects of customer service. But this more expedient approach can harm customer relations. It also tends to de-emphasize the customer service values most important to staff members, who find fulfillment in the personal quality of relationships and in adapting services for individuals. For example, a bank may emphasize the use of ATM machines only because the cost per transaction is lower than the cost of an interaction with a teller. Financial considerations constrict the range of services without regard for the needs of customers. The efficiency value overshadows the other service values.

Not Doing What We Say

In addition to conflict over the choice of service values, employees are distressed by insincerity in organizational values. People who work as a front-line staff must take the brunt of complaints from disgruntled customers. They have the job of making excuses for policies they may disagree with. They rarely see a direct benefit to themselves in the money being saved by the organization when it downgrades the depth of its services. Instead they are painfully aware of the shortfall in services for the customer and the constraints on their own career development.

Genuine agreement on central values, difficult as it is to attain, is not enough. Even when everyone accepts the wording of an organizational mission statement, they will encounter serious problems in implementation, especially when money is tight. Cost-cutting measures are often directly at odds with enhancing quality of care and the welfare of staff members. Here's what one retail salesperson told us: "The company's stated goals are at great odds with actual practice. Goals and values sound nice, but often go by the wayside due to budget constraints and convenience. Customer service has been gradually deteriorating due to diminished staffing and increased busywork. Staff morale is poor because changes are made with seemingly no thought to how they affect customer service. The staff are providing fewer services even though they are working harder. This job is so money oriented that a lot of the human aspects of the job just go to the bottom of the priority list."

To some extent there is a mismatch between means and ends because the value clarification process is incomplete. The process often stops at the formulation of a global mission. Organizational missions and objectives are fairly abstract, lofty concepts, whereas the strategies for attaining them are the stuff of day-to-day work life. A change in strategy has a more immediate impact on an individual's workday than does a change in the organization's mission. Strategies are also closer to the political dimension of organizational life. Managers do not allocate staff and resources to objectives per se but rather to strategies for pursuing them. It is in the strategies that managers state their values concerning how the organization operates.

When an abstract value is translated into a concrete strategy, it often fails to recognize the diverse interpretations of these values by different people throughout the organization. You and each of your colleagues interpret organizational values from the perspective of your personal experience and your immediate work setting. You are psychologically involved in your job on a local level, in terms of your day-to-day interactions with the people with whom you work. Accommodating the values of diverse work settings throughout an organization is beyond the strategic planning perspectives of most organizations. But it is a necessary step toward integrating an organization and promoting engagement with work. Here is an example:

> Sam is a loans officer in a rural bank branch. He experienced the limits of his capacity to implement strategies consistent with his values at work. The central office decreed that all branches reduce costs by reducing the hours tellers work each week and by changing their weekday closing time from 5 P.M. to 3 P.M. For the central office, this decision was a matter with which every branch had to comply. But Sam saw this move as contrary to customer service, because late afternoon was his branch's peak business time. It was also inconsistent with maintaining the level of personal and business loans, because new loan customers generally came from that same customer base.
>
> The lack of a genuine commitment to the bank's stated customer service values frustrated Sam and other people at the branch. This conflict increased their vulnerability to burnout: it exhausted emotional energy, reduced their involvement in the work, and decreased their sense of effectiveness.

With organizational missions and strategies changing and often conflicting, it is not surprising that people often work at cross-purposes. Their goals cannot be achieved in their day-to-day operations. As one orthopedic surgeon put it, "You get into this craft to do good things for people and practice to the best of your ability, but we can't do that anymore." This doctor is not unique in seeing his organization as progressing from being merely ineffective to actively thwarting his capacity to do his job. The management of his hospital, however, believes that it is doing everything possible to support his work despite major reductions in the funding received from the government. The surgeon is aware that ultimately his conflict is with the government, but the conflicts occur locally. The hospital administrators who are scrambling to keep things functioning with fewer resources are the immediate target of his discontent.

A large number of well-intentioned, talented, and dedicated people find themselves stuck. They cannot bring about the organizational world they desire, yet they cannot simply shrug off this experience as a minor shortcoming. It strikes to the heart of their relationship with their work.

WHERE DO WE GO FROM HERE?

My, isn't all this depressing! Perhaps we should just chuck all of this work nonsense and spend more time with our loved ones at home. Setting up a small crafts business and operating on the barter system in a rural community seems to be the only reasonable alternative.

But wait. That alternative neglects the whole motivational background that gets people in trouble with work in the first place. People like to be involved in projects that go beyond themselves. They want to develop their effectiveness by taking on challenges that make demands on all of their abilities and require a full commitment of their physical, emotional, and creative energy. If these things were not important, we would not be discussing burnout in the first place. People would go to work, make money, go home, and have a good time. The work-for-money framework is an incomplete one, as is limiting yourself entirely to personal interactions. Spending more time at home and developing indifference toward work is not a solution.

It remains that people have created organizations as environments in which they can work together to further what they value. That organizations have become twisted out of shape in the midst of major transitions in the nature of work does not mean that they are defunct. They are a valuable resource to be protected, developed, and nurtured. It is not reasonable to relinquish organizations to those who wish to exploit them for their short-term money-generating capacity. The challenge is to take charge of organizational life, not to escape from it. In the next chapter we talk about how to do just that.

4

Why Do Anything About Burnout?

Even though burnout has been identified as a problem in the workplace, not everybody agrees that it is a problem that has to be taken seriously. For various reasons, burnout is downplayed or dismissed as an inevitable—but manageable—part of working life.

Dave, the CEO of an insurance company, admits feeling dubious about burnout. "People are always grumbling about burnout. I've certainly felt burned out myself after a long stretch of meetings and business trips. But it's a problem people have to deal with. The employer is obligated to pay a decent wage and to provide reasonable working conditions. It's not the employer's responsibility to make everybody happy."

Dave has made it clear to his human resource department that he does not want them putting time into burnout or job stress. The company has a contract with a counseling firm for an employee assistance program (EAP). That should be sufficient to deal with whatever personal problems people bring to work.

"The thing about burnout is that it is a problem for the individual," says Dave. "It does not have any real impact on the organization's productivity. It is a soft problem, not a clear-cut matter of finance or strategic management. So, if people want to use the EAP program or take their vacation days to get a good rest, that's fine. That's what those things are there for. There's not much else the organization can do. If people can't take the heat, maybe they will get burned out enough that they will just leave on their own, and I won't have to go through the trouble of firing them. People have to do what is necessary to look after themselves. I've got a company to run."

WHY ORGANIZATIONS IGNORE BURNOUT

Dave is not unique. Managers have often been reluctant to address burnout among staff members. They have seen burnout as a can of worms that is best left unopened. They fear that once they acknowledge burnout, they will be overwhelmed by demands from staff members to cut workload or to initiate costly "quality of work life" programs. They do not see burnout as the employer's responsibility. And they are unconvinced that they could do anything about burnout even if they had the money, time, and expertise to devote to the problem. Let's look a little more closely at the underlying assumptions here.

"It's a Problem for the Individual"

As we saw in Chapter Two, the common response to burnout is to blame the person. If you're feeling burned out, then it is you who has a problem. Maybe you're letting difficulties at home interfere with the job. Maybe you've got an attitude problem—always complaining about everyone else but not taking responsibility for your own actions. Maybe you haven't got the right stuff—you're just not good enough or tough enough to handle the work. Whatever the particular diagnosis, it remains an individual one.

And if it is an individual problem, then individual solutions are the logical answer. Whatever your difficulty, or flaw, or weakness—that's what needs to be fixed. To do that, you usually have to get rest, or get help, or get out. Getting rest is likely to mean taking time off, going on vacation, or developing a more relaxed lifestyle. Getting help usually means learning new skills, improving your health, or seeking counseling or another type of treatment. Getting out means leaving the job entirely.

There are many variations of these basic individual strategies, which go under the general rubric of stress management. You can buy books on this topic and try the techniques on your own. Or you may have access to workshops or seminars on stress management; many organizations provide this kind of benefit to their employees.

This focus on the person and on helping oneself fits in with our society's individualistic philosophy. In this view, people are responsible for their own outcomes. They can take credit for their successes but have only themselves to blame for their failures. This philosophy also celebrates the triumph of the individual over any obstacle. People must meet the challenge head-on, make it over the hurdle—not eliminate the hurdle itself. When this view is applied to burnout, it means learning how to deal with the stressors on the job rather than figuring out how to get rid of them to create a stress-free environment.

"It's Not the Employer's Responsibility"

If burnout is the individual's problem, then by definition it is not the organization's problem. It is the individual's responsibility to figure out how to adapt successfully to the work situation. It is not the employer's responsibility to figure out how to adapt the job to you or to any of your colleagues.

From this perspective, does burnout ever become an organizational problem? Yes, if it begins to involve major loss of income. But the organization feels obligated to do something only after a demonstrated problem, not before. There is no point in spending money until it's absolutely necessary. In terms of keeping down costs, it's both easier and cheaper to focus on changing individual employees than on changing the entire organization.

"It Doesn't Have Any Real Impact on the Organization"

Even if individual employees are burned out, it is not seen as cause for alarm in the organization. Why? Because the organization does not see how it affects the bottom-line performance. Employees keep showing up and doing their jobs. If feeling burned out causes them to quit, it will avoid the personal unpleasantness and legal liabilities associated with dismissal. Employees don't get sick or injured because of burnout. They don't die because of burnout. Burnout does not violate the law, so the organization does not risk exposure to costly litigation. Reducing psychological stressors is not required for occupational health and safety in the same way that controlling hazard and infection is.

From this viewpoint, burnout does not make much of a financial dent in the organization. So what's to worry about? If employees let their emotions interfere with their work, then the employer can deal with the problem in the same way as any other performance problems. Burnout is not so prevalent or unique that it can't be handled by standard procedures and programs that are already in place.

"There's Not Much the Organization Can Do"

In this view, the best the organization can do about burnout is simply allow people to look after themselves. Through rest, counseling, and personal initiative, people can do whatever is necessary to address this problem. The organization may try to help them change and cope more effectively by providing special programs or workshops but ultimately the solution is up to them.

Thus, the organization has your best interests at heart but takes a hands-off approach to achieving them. There is a bit of a benevolent paternalism at work here—if you are unable to take care of yourself, the organization may try to point you in the right direction and see if you can figure things out on your own. But the implicit message is that the organization is helpless. It's not that organizations don't want to do something about burnout, but rather that they truly don't know what would make a difference.

WHY ORGANIZATIONS SHOULD TAKE BURNOUT SERIOUSLY

In fact, all of these assumptions are off the mark. They minimize what is actually a very significant problem, and they pass the buck on its solutions. It is a critical mistake to adopt this viewpoint and ignore burnout. Burnout *does* affect the organization's bottom line. It is not just an individual problem but much more than that. It is the employer's responsibility to improve the organization, and it turns out that organizations *can* do a lot about burnout.

Burnout Affects the Bottom Line

The bottom-line argument about burnout is that it doesn't affect the organization's performance. Nothing could be further from the truth. In fact, job stress can lead to substantial financial and productivity loss, and anyone who is unaware of this basic fact has been in denial for quite some time.

At this point, we could present the usual general statistics that show how many billions of dollars are being swallowed up by workers' compensation, health care benefits (particularly for mental health and substance abuse), absenteeism, sick leave, and employee fraud, not to mention the losses incurred because of on-the-job error and deteriorating quality of work. Although these big numbers could underscore the financial enormity of the problem, they could not convey the process by which burnout translates into big bucks. So let's take each of the job-person mismatches that contribute to burnout and see how, in actual cases, it affects the bottom line.[9]

WORK OVERLOAD

When a food-processing company restructured, it asked Anita, one of its best district managers, to take over the management of the new consolidated area. These new responsibilities were so extensive that Anita's workweek increased from fifty-five to seventy hours. She soon began to experience the feelings of exhaustion, cynicism, and ineffectiveness that are characteristic of burnout. She told her supervisor that the new district was too large for her to manage, but he made no effort to accommodate her need for assistance or job restructuring.

Anita tried to deal with her burnout by getting psychiatric treatment, but it was not very successful. Eventually, she filed for workers' compensation benefits for her psychiatric injury. Although the company challenged the claim, Anita proved that her burnout was a reaction to abnormal working conditions and she won her case. Thus, the costs to the company for its failure to deal with the mismatch in work overload included quite a list: long-term workers' compensation benefits to Anita; payment for her psychiatric treatment prior to the claim; legal fees; recruitment and training costs associated with filling her position when she left it; loss of revenue and loss of long-term customers caused by disruptions in sales activity in her district; and adverse publicity generated by her case.

LACK OF CONTROL

Bob was a customer service representative for a government agency. His job offered a classic example of lack of control: he was in the public view daily, dealing with large numbers of people who were frustrated by the long lines and bureaucratic red tape, and who became angry and belligerent when Bob had to deny them the financial benefits they sought for their claims. Things got even worse when Congressional legislation changed the rules of the operating policies. Even though Bob had no say in what the rules should be, he had to carry them out and justify them to an irate public.

Over time, Bob developed a serious case of burnout. His anger and frustration were often expressed in fights with his supervisor and in rudeness toward his clients, many of whom filed formal complaints. He began to experience hypertension—not uncommon among men with demanding jobs that give them little control over their work. Bob's growing alienation from his work led to greater absenteeism—twice the average—and he also began to drink heavily.

The cost to the agency of Bob's burnout was considerable: in addition to the cost of his absenteeism, his health care expenses were five times higher than the average, several of his errors on the job cost the agency thousands of dollars, and his visible fights with management had a negative impact on the morale of his co-workers.

INSUFFICIENT REWARD

In an attempt to contain health care costs, a hospital cut its nurses' salaries by 15 percent. Not surprisingly, the nurses were outraged by this loss of income and went out on strike. The hospital brought in some nonunion nurses and took a tough bargaining stance with union leaders. Eventually the strike ended, but the nurses had had to accept a salary cut of 10 percent.

During the next year, many of the nurses complained of burnout—of working too hard and too long for too little pay and very little respect—and they began to leave for other jobs. Several of the departing nurses were the most senior and experienced, and their replacements lacked both their expertise and their familiarity with the hospital's procedures. Mistakes were made, patients complained, and some malpractice suits were filed. As morale deteriorated, more nurses quit, while those who remained with the hospital carried chips on their shoulders.

Although the hospital had saved money in the short-term by lowering salaries, the end result was the loss of its best staff to burnout, and the negative effect of that loss went far beyond the costs of simply replacing them.

BREAKDOWN OF COMMUNITY

A manufacturing company was organized into different work teams of five to fifteen people, with each team responsible for establishing its own practices. However, there was no process for effectively handling disagreements, as is common in self-directed work team environments.

After a while, several teams began to have problems. Escalating conflicts between team colleagues created a very unpleasant working climate, and burnout was the result. Everyone became so tense and irritable that tempers flared over minor problems, and the bickering and grumbling were constant. At times this behavior was so bad that it brought productivity to a halt. It also derailed company efforts to implement a new quality control system. The lack of trust and the chronic hostility made it almost impossible for team colleagues to collaborate effectively. Although the new system was eventually implemented, it took six years rather than the two originally expected.

ABSENCE OF FAIRNESS

A large energy company instituted a system of new controls to produce greater efficiency and fewer errors, offering incentive bonuses to employees who proposed new techniques for further improvement. The new controls were enforced by managers who roamed the halls looking for infractions. As a result, the work culture became stark and regimented, almost like a boot camp. And employees who wanted the bonuses would sometimes cheat, claiming that an old technique was their own "new" idea.

Burnout was rampant, and (according to an internal survey) it was due primarily to perceived unfairness. Employees felt that there was a lack of basic respect, as well as unethical behaviors to exploit the system for personal gain and unfair distribution of rewards. The bitter feelings among many employees led them to pull out from the job or to retaliate. People no longer put in extra effort when it was needed but did only the bare minimum instead. They failed to report violations of safe work procedures. Absenteeism increased, and there were incidents of sabotage and pilfering. Health care costs for stress-related problems went up, as did the number of disability cases.

CONFLICTING VALUES

A nonprofit social service agency faced a number of internal problems related to values. It had never had a clearly articulated mission or coherent strategic plan but instead expanded to offer a particular service whenever an opportunity arose to generate some revenue. Thus, it offered five different client services but had no integrated service delivery system. Many members of the board of directors were allied with one of the five services exclusively, and so they would fight to get a bigger chunk of the budget for "their" service rather than concern themselves with the overall welfare of the agency. Even the chief operating officer had trouble making fair and dispassionate decisions for the agency as a whole because she was biased in favor of one of the services.

Ongoing conflicts over the agency's values, goals, and programs led to chaos in its daily operation and burnout among the staff. Money was wasted as funding sources were shifted around unpredictably. Projects were started but not completed. As a result of the high levels of anxiety and frustration among the burned-out staff, health care benefits were constantly used (particularly for employee counseling), absenteeism and tardiness were high, morale plummeted, and the quality of customer service deteriorated. Meaningful change and a sense of purpose only came about after the near-total turnover of the board and staff members.

Burnout Is More Than Just an Individual Problem

Clearly, burnout comes at a heavy price. It is not just a trivial matter of people feeling cranky or having bad days—burnout costs money. And this economic bottom line can only be controlled by paying attention to the human bottom line. It is behavior in the workplace that is either costly or productive. An effective strategy of behavioral risk management has to understand not only what the behaviors are but why they occur.

Unfortunately, the goal of understanding "people's behavior" is too often misinterpreted as understanding "people's problems." In turn, that fosters a focus on the person rather than on the situation and the assumption that burnout is the fault of the individual. As we've already argued, that interpretation is incorrect. It is not the person alone, but the *mismatch* between the person and the job environment that is critical. A person's behavior in the workplace can only be understood when it is examined within the social context of that workplace.

This misguided focus on the person alone is a primary reason why the majority of stress management techniques are designed to change the individual, but not the situation. In addition, organizations consider most programs targeting personal change—such as workshops—to be low cost. They don't impinge much, if at all, on the organization's daily operation, and they are relatively inexpensive.

But as it turns out, these low-cost individual strategies yield a low return on the investment. Their track record for producing noticeable improvements with regard to burnout is not very impressive. From our perspective, a key reason why they are relatively ineffective is precisely *because* they don't impinge on the organization. It is ironic that they focus on changing the person and not the job when research shows that the job is the critical source of stress. Another drawback of these programs that focus on the individual is that they often come across as demeaning and patronizing to those who take them. The implicit message is, "You don't know how to take care of yourself, so we'll have to show you."

> Carolyn is a public school teacher, and her response to employee assistance programs is not atypical. "Every summer, just before school starts, the district comes up with some sort of program to 'motivate' us. Last year, we were given a workshop on stress reduction, which wasn't at all helpful. In fact, it was offensive—because it was saying that the stress was 'all in me,' so I should just 'exercise and take a walk to reduce stress.' What about only getting a 1 percent pay raise over five years! There's where stress is, and exercising every day is not a solution!"

Even when people recognize that the problem involves more than just the individual, they may still make the mistake of assuming that they can handle it all by themselves. In fact, burnout is a bigger problem than any one person can manage. Although you may be able to change your own behavior, you cannot single-handedly change your social environment. Reducing mismatches in workload, control, community, or fairness requires the involvement of many people within a work group and across an organization. Changing things at work is never an individual process, but a group one.

Suzanne, a special education teacher in a public school, had burned out in her work with learning-disabled students. She decided that what she needed was to change her teaching technique so that she could work more effectively with fewer students. After receiving initial encouragement from the principal, she signed up for training with a consulting team during her summer vacation.

Suzanne returned to school in September feeling optimistic and excited about her job for the first time in a long while. But before the week was out, her program was in shambles. The new approach had a solid track record, but it was based on intensive individual work with students. To accomplish it, Suzanne had to work with only a fifth of the number of students she had worked with the previous year. Furthermore, the ninety-minute sessions around which the program was structured conflicted with the school's one-hour class schedule, so her students had to return to their regular classes halfway through the lesson or leave their regular classes before they were over.

The other teachers complained to Suzanne and to the principal. Parents whose children were on the waiting list for Suzanne's classes called the school daily. The principal let Suzanne know that he was concerned not only with these complaints but also with how the drop in the special education statistics would be viewed by the school's district office. Suzanne knew it was impossible to adapt her new method to a larger group setting, but the principal made it clear that she had no choice. She would have to see more students and she would have to conform to the school's schedule.

Suzanne had initiated what appeared to be a solid intervention to deal with burnout. She had developed expertise that would permit her to control her workload and to do a more effective job. Within the context of her work, the intervention made perfect sense. But within the broader context of the school and the community, it was impossible.

What went wrong for Suzanne? The central lesson here is that changing things at work is never a purely personal endeavor. You may be a unique individual but at work you are also fulfilling a role that is related to the roles of other people. Any meaningful change at work has an impact on those other people, and they will want to be involved in the process of change as well. Furthermore, those other people may well share your concerns and may want to make the same change as you do and for similar reasons.

The six mismatches between people and the job are organizational issues. Management policies determine workload and specify the amount of control people may exercise over their work. The organization's sense of community, the way in which it rewards its members, and its sense of fairness or respect are shared qualities of its social environments. These are not individual qualities, although they are important factors in the work life of individuals. The organization's values, the sincerity with which it pursues those values, its tolerance for diverse perspectives among its membership—these are all organizational qualities, not qualities of the individuals who work there.

Addressing Burnout Improves the Organization

Our argument is that burnout is best addressed at the organizational level rather than the individual one. Such action does not necessarily reflect an altruistic motive on the part of employers; indeed, it is a matter of self-interest. By taking responsibility for dealing with burnout, the organization will be managing in a way that will ensure it has a productive staff for the long term.

Why is this so? As we have seen, the experience of burnout is incompatible with effective work, especially when the work involves relating to other people or generating creative ideas. People need to be engaged in this kind of work to do it well, because these activities demand energy, involvement, and self-confidence. Here are some examples:

- Developing computer software is a process of creative problem solving. Software designers need mental energy to concentrate on the many pieces of a complex problem. They need the capacity to get involved in the project, to keep the challenges in mind day after day, and to think of new approaches to problems. They need to be engaged with their work. A company must offer an emotional climate that supports its staff in order to succeed in this competitive industry.

- The most powerful predictor of patient satisfaction in a hospital is the relationship with the nurse on the ward. Attentive, capable nursing has a direct impact on the patients' sense of well-being and their healing. In critical care nursing, life-threatening problems that require sophisticated solutions and focused action arise quickly. A hospital is more productive when organizational practices support energetic and involved nursing.

- Students know when teachers are burned out. They see the teachers' impatience, inattention to their work, and lack of personal support for their efforts. A school that does not help its teachers remain engaged with their work makes less of a contribution to student learning.

An organization that supports engagement with work is a stronger organization that is better able to respond to its clientele, grow in new and exciting ways, and develop creative ideas or products. In contrast, an organization in which people are experiencing burnout is less able to accept major change in its environment and in its own structures or procedures. Burnout saps creativity and erodes the capacity to work effectively with customers or colleagues.

Organizations need to take the initiative in dealing with burnout for another, related reason as well. Contrary to the popular wisdom espoused at the beginning of this chapter by Dave the CEO, people experiencing burnout do not always quit. This is more true now, during the current crisis in the job environment, than it was in previous years when job opportunities were more plentiful and people felt that they had choices. Today, employees who are burned out may remain on the job, making minimal contributions, feeling tired and cynical, and limiting the potential of their work group. An organization can't ignore this problem if it is concerned about productivity. As long as these people stick around, an organization will have to deal with them for its own good.

Organizations Can Do a Lot

Organizations are not usually seen as helpless creatures that are unable to solve the problems they face. So the argument that organizations simply can't do very much about this type of job stress seems odd. On the contrary, organizations have the power and the resources to do a great deal. An organizational approach to burnout and engagement has great potential for bringing about effective change. Here's why:

1.   An organizational approach addresses the problems of a group of people instead of focusing on one individual at a time. As a result, the approach is not only more cost-effective but also builds in mutually supportive processes, because colleagues with whom staff members interact also benefit from the intervention. An intervention that builds mutual respect among colleagues enhances engagement with work for the work group.

2.   By improving overall human resource management, an organizational approach enhances productivity as well as the quality

of staff members' work life. For example, a financial advisor who is feeling engaged with his work will search out information more thoroughly and attend more closely to his clients.

3. An intervention at the organizational level that enhances the functioning of a work setting has a better chance of promoting job engagement. In contrast, when an intervention is at the individual level, the goal is usually to return a distressed person to a "baseline" level of functioning (that is, the state of not being burned out), but it rarely goes beyond this to become proactive.

Despite its value, an organizational approach is more complex and therefore more challenging. Because people tend to think of events as being caused by individuals rather than by groups or social processes, it's not easy to conceive of an intervention in organizational terms. It can be difficult to identify the precise target of an organizational intervention, and this ambiguity makes it harder to implement changes that will affect an organization's social environment. Even more problematic is that such interventions can disrupt management processes and power structures, so they tend to generate automatic resistance. Here is an example of an organizational intervention, with its problems and successes:

> Managers in an aircraft maintenance shop noted that some technicians took considerably longer than the average to complete standard sections of the safety check of aircraft. They considered a system that fined individuals who performed too slowly but then rejected the approach because they feared it would encourage cursory safety checks for which the aircraft industry had little tolerance.
>
> Instead, they implemented a team approach to safety checks in which the entire team's time for completing the safety check was monitored rather than the performance of individuals. This intervention shifted the responsibility for monitoring efficiency to the work team. In the early days of the new procedure, team leaders complained to managers that they were unable to track

what was happening in their teams or to take corrective action when overall performance was not up to standard. Thus, the first effect of the intervention was not to speed up the safety check but to cause distress among team members.

The managers provided the teams with a brief series of team-building workshops that helped the members work more effectively with one another. The teams developed a shared sense of the overall task and learned to accommodate the pace of their work in a way that permitted safety checks that were thorough but not too time consuming.

In this intervention, the target shifted from the individual to the group. Rather than singling out individuals and pressuring them to increase their pace, the intervention encouraged teamwork while co-workers developed a manageable but effective approach to the job. Similarly, organizational approaches to addressing burnout are more effective when they are integrated into strategic management policies than when they are directed at problematic individuals.

WHY IT'S BETTER TO PREVENT BURNOUT NOW THAN DEAL WITH IT LATER

As we pointed out in Chapter One, according to the popular lore about problems in the workplace, "If it ain't broke, don't fix it." In other words, don't bother doing anything about a potential problem, wait until there is a real problem. This approach focuses on short-term gains rather than future benefits. The inherent gamble is that the potential problem will never materialize, so the organization "wins" by not spending money to avoid what could be a phantom.

We believe that this gamble is far too risky when it comes to burnout. First of all, the likelihood of burnout is too great—it's no longer a rare event. Second, as we saw earlier in this chapter, once burnout becomes a real problem, it is enormously expensive. The financial costs, the reduced productivity, the health problems, the decline in overall quality of life—all of this is a very high price to pay. Third, it is harder to deal effectively with burnout when it is a full-blown problem than when it is incipient. At the later stage, treatment is difficult and the organization is faced with major damage control.

Thus, the countertruism we advocate is, "An ounce of prevention is worth a pound of cure." A preventive approach involves a long-range vision, not a short-term one. This approach holds that making an investment in the present will forestall much greater costs and losses in the future. This approach "wins" because it spends less in the long run by heading off the worst effects of the problem. For example, paying for job training now will prevent the costs of poor performance later. Hiring another staff member now—rather than having one person handle a double load—will prevent a deterioration in the quality of the work and avoid the costs of exhaustion and illness. Developing a procedure for resolving team conflicts will prevent future conflicts that could interfere with productivity. Getting input and feedback from workers before policy changes go into effect will prevent resistance and unanticipated problems. And so on and so on.

In our opinion, the best way to prevent burnout is to promote engagement with work. It is not simply a matter of reducing the negatives in the workplace; it is also an attempt to increase the positives. Strategies for developing engagement with work are those that enhance energy, involvement, and efficacy, and we will look at these in more depth later on in the book.

Most important, a preventive approach represents a wise and prudent investment in the future of the organization. It means investing in people so that they become well-trained, loyal, and dedicated employees who can be counted on to do high-quality work. This kind of investment will strengthen the organization for future survival. In unpredictable times of crisis and chaos, such employees are essential for managing transitions and change and steering the organization into a new global reality. Thus, the critical return on the investment is a human one, not simply a short-term economic gain.

An investment of this sort requires a reciprocal arrangement between employers and employees. The organization has to be able to show the same kind of commitment to its employees—the respect and concern—that it asks of them. The best way for an organization to do this is by taking steps to minimize the six mismatches between people and their jobs. For a number of organizational leaders, this kind of approach makes perfect sense. Unlike our CEO Dave, they see the prevention of burnout as critical to the well-being of their workplace. Lee, a CEO who runs a major hospital, put it this way: "I am convinced that organizations that manage themselves on the basis of open, honest communication, respect for the people who work there and for the people they serve, and a concern for quality care will outperform other organizations in the long run. If I am wrong, I would rather go back to practicing family medicine than be CEO of a hospital."

We realize that this is not the mode of operation in much of the workplace. And we know that we may sound naive and idealistic when we advocate investing in people and taking a preventive approach. Nevertheless, we believe strongly that this is the path that will lead us away from burnout and toward productive engagement with work.

So it is clear that the goal is to minimize the mismatches, but how do people go about reaching it? In fact, there is a process that can promote progress toward that goal—and it can start either at the individual level, with a person committed to change, or at the organizational level, with management that is equally committed. In the next two chapters we'll describe just which actions are necessary to get that process going, and thus to reduce the likelihood of burnout.

5

Crisis Intervention to Stop Burnout

Do things seem to be reaching a crisis point at work? Is burnout becoming a serious problem? Does the situation seem to be overwhelming? Do you ever wish there was something that somebody could do about it? Well, take heart—there are ways that one person can take action against burnout, and that one person could well be you.

Our message here is not going to be the one you've probably heard from various self-help books and programs—about how you can take charge of your life, get yourself in shape, and lead yourself to happiness. It's not that we're knocking self-improvement. Taking care of yourself is definitely a good thing to do, and there are lots of options for strengthening both your physical and mental well-being. But you can learn about these options elsewhere, and so we won't repeat them here.

Rather, our point is that self-improvement alone is not enough to beat burnout. To resolve the mismatches between person and job, it is necessary to focus on *both* the individual and the workplace, not just the person alone. As we have argued throughout this book, the sources of burnout are more situational than personal, so solutions to the problem need to be sought within the social context of the workplace.

What we are going to do in this chapter and the next is present a problem-solving process for burnout. In this chapter we'll show

how the process is used in a crisis mode; in Chapter Six we'll demonstrate how it is used for prevention. Figure 5.1 illustrates the two approaches that may be taken in the problem-solving process.

This problem-solving process takes as its starting point any one of the six mismatches between person and job. It focuses on both person and job by linking specific conditions in the workplace to the individual's emotions and work behaviors. It looks at how potential changes will affect the three dimensions of burnout—exhaustion, cynicism, and ineffectiveness—and promote movement toward its opposite—engagement. The process is social and collaborative, and it strives to enhance communication between people and the organization. And, we emphasize, it is an ongoing *process*— not a quick fix and not a superficial, happy-ever-after ending.

This process can be used either for crisis management or for prevention. In the former case, burnout is the present reality; in the latter case, it is likely in the future. In crisis management the goal is to find immediate solutions to alleviate the problem. Prevention, in contrast, takes a more long-term perspective on strategies that will

FIGURE 5.1. Two Approaches to the Problem-Solving Process.

Individual Approach

It starts with a person

↓

It becomes a group project

↓

It connects to the organization

Organizational Approach

It starts with management

↓

It becomes an organizational project

↓

It connects to people

The outcome affects related mismatches

↓

The outcome is a process

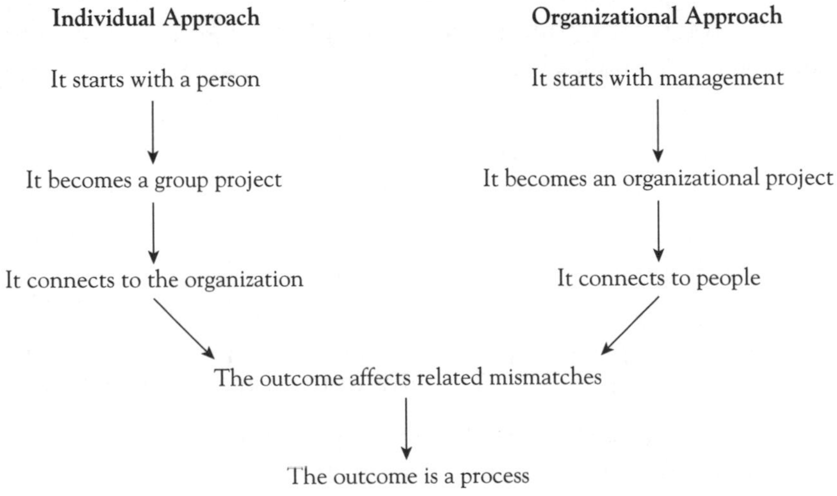

reduce future risks and promote future growth. However, in both instances the overall problem-solving process is basically the same: the problem is a particular mismatch and the solution needs to connect the job setting to individual employees.

So how does this process begin? As we said, it can be initiated by either an individual or an organization. When individual workers start the ball rolling, it is usually because the job situation has reached a crisis point for them and their colleagues. Burnout has become a major issue and nothing is being done at the organizational level to resolve it, so people begin to take action on their own. Instead of withdrawing or quitting, an individual can inspire a larger work group to tackle the problem of a particular mismatch and generate some initial solutions. In contrast, when the process starts at the organizational level it is more often an attempt to prevent burnout in the future than to respond to a crisis. Management recognizes the potential costs of burnout and decides to take action to contain them. This is not to say that organizations don't initiate crisis-management processes or that individuals don't initiate preventive actions—obviously, that can happen too—but the opposite pattern is more typical, and so that is how we will present the processes in this book.

TAKING ON THE JOB-PERSON MISMATCH INDIVIDUALLY

Even if burnout seems to be a much bigger problem than any one person can handle, that doesn't mean you should give in to it or not even try to do something about it. Individuals can take action to start the process of stopping burnout. All you need are the following things:

- An understanding of the six paths from mismatch to burnout
- An ability to work with colleagues
- A commitment to stick with the process of change

This book has helped you to understand what burnout is and what makes it happen. The six ways in which people and their jobs are mismatched are the critical sources of burnout, and so any analysis of the problem has to address them.

The ability to work with others is essential because going it alone is rarely effective. The fact is, you do not work in isolation. Your job is interrelated with the jobs others are doing, so that whatever affects your work will have a ripple effect on everyone else. Given that the workplace is increasingly a shared enterprise, you will have to work together with your colleagues in order to deal effectively with burnout.

Change takes time, particularly when it's a question of a long-term, chronic problem like burnout. That means you have to be committed, persistent, and patient, and stick with the process until it yields some progress.

There are several key steps in the process to stop burnout. We'll describe them briefly, in general terms, so that you will be able to recognize them easily in the three case studies that follow.

Step 1: It Starts with a Person

The process begins when a person prompts a work group to consider its problems with burnout and its need for solutions. This individual impetus to deal with burnout does not need to come from a person in charge. Often, formal authority interferes with a person's capacity to provide effective leadership. But no matter who it is, that person has to take a leadership role. That means doing the necessary background work, getting the group involved, and leading the group through the process. The challenge is to inspire a group to take direct action that improves the situation.

Step 2: It Becomes a Group Project

One person can begin the process, but a group is necessary to develop and sustain it. To correct factors in the workplace the combined efforts of the work group are necessary. People have to reach a consensus about the area of mismatch they need to address first, and then prioritize the actions they will take to address it. They have to support one another in those actions, and work to maintain the momentum for change.

Step 3: It Connects to the Organization

Whatever the solutions proposed to deal with burnout, they cannot be implemented in a vacuum. Even though the interventions may be initiated by an individual or a group, they have to be implemented within the organizational context.

Step 4: The Outcome Affects Related Mismatches

Addressing the six areas of mismatch that we have identified in this book is the only way to make an impact on burnout and foster effective engagement with work. This does not mean that every action must address all six mismatches simultaneously—the process is easier and clearer when it focuses on just one. However, the six organizational areas in which mismatches occur are somewhat interrelated so that action on any of them tends to improve at least some of the others.

Step 5: The Outcome Is a Process

The basic message here is that the important outcome is not a "happy ending" but an ongoing process of successful adaptation to an ever-evolving workplace. It is not necessary to address every aspect of a complex change process deliberately. Once the process begins, it gathers its own momentum toward change and improvement.

Now that we've outlined the steps in the process, let's see them put to good use. We'll revisit three of the people we introduced in Chapter One and see how they used the process to deal with a particular mismatch that was leading to burnout. In Eleanor's case the mismatch was work overload, for Stan it was lack of control, and for John it was insufficient rewards.

TRYING TO REDUCE WORK OVERLOAD

As we saw in Chapter One, Eleanor could not meet the ever-growing demands of her job as a manager of an automobile claims adjustment department in a large insurance company. She knew the limits of her energy and her commitment to life outside of work, but she felt vulnerable to losing her job if her performance fell short. In spite of placing increasing demands on her, central management had given her a directive to reduce the number of staff in her unit. Eleanor had enough experience in the industry and with her staff members to know that the current workload was unsustainable.

It Starts with a Person

The solution was not obvious to Eleanor, but she knew that she had to work with her department to find a new balance between energy and demands. She came to the group prepared. First, she met with the vice president to review the company's strategy and the role her department was to play in establishing a stronger position in a more competitive insurance world. Second, she went over reports analyzing the costs and benefits for her department. Third, she examined industry reports on innovations in claims adjustment work, noting new industry standards and practices. She then prepared a synopsis of her background work and distributed it to department members just prior to their meeting to discuss plans and strategies.

It Becomes a Group Project

The meeting began with three people expressing their strong dissatisfaction with the current state of affairs. They felt the strain of exhaustion and the frustration of doing rushed and incomplete work. They felt that the company was putting them in jeopardy by insisting on a rate of claims management that did not permit a thorough examination of the facts.

Eleanor steered the discussion to the values that the staff held about their work. The first value mentioned was attentiveness to clients, who are often distressed when contacting an insurance claims office. A second value was thoroughness and accuracy. Third, the group members were committed to efficient, effective action. Fourth, they were determined to be responsive to the individual customer. Each of these four values made demands on the time, energy, and resources of the work group.

Eleanor then asked the group to consider how their current workload interfered with their abiding by these values. People had no trouble coming up with examples of incidents in which time pressures forced them to cut corners when interpreting policies or making investigations. Although there were no clear-cut cases of successful fraudulent claims over the past six months, there were a number of cases in which the agent felt less than confident about a claim's validity. The group calculated that the total liability for those questionable claims exceeded the salary of five staff members. The group noted an increase in the frequency and intensity of strained interactions with clients, and saw these problems as resulting directly from the rushed state of affairs in the office.

Eleanor asked the group to look at the problem as a matter of choice. The reduction in staff coupled with an increase in caseload meant that remaining workers had to put less time and energy than previously into each case. So one solution to the problem was to find more time to maintain the level of staff involvement in cases by finding efficiencies outside of casework. But the staff members were convinced that the initiatives they had taken earlier in the year had boosted overall office efficiency as far as it could go. Another strategy was to give up personal time—work late and arrive early—in order to maintain high-quality service. But this was their current solution, and it was not working.

Eleanor proposed that the group could take control of the workload situation by choosing to emphasize some values over others. After a lengthy discussion the group chose to emphasize personal and responsive service. Eleanor took on the task of working with two staff members to write a statement of the department's commitment to these values.

It Connects to the Organization

Eleanor also wrote a proposal to the vice president on the financial impact of delayed or less-than-thorough investigations. She estimated the ongoing costs to the company of rushed investigations and indicated that adding two staff positions in her department would be a cost-effective way for the department to regain its previous levels of accuracy and efficiency.

Although this solution meant that the group had to adapt to the current state of things, it also involved a communication outside of the group to the vice president emphasizing the estimated cost of possibly fraudulent claims and requesting additional resources. By requesting additional staff, Eleanor brought the larger organization into the group's deliberations on values: Did the organization consider their values to be worthy of attention? If the organization made a clear commitment to the group's customer service values, it would support their efforts to address the customer demands they had to deal with. Without such a commitment, the group might find itself attempting to pursue customer service values that were no longer important to the organization. Communicating with the larger organization provides a broader context in which to develop a response to an area of mismatch.

Eleanor worked out the costs of de-emphasizing accuracy and thoroughness. She used records from two previous years to estimate the number of fraudulent claims that had been identified thanks to her staff's thorough investigations and projected the cost to the company of their conducting more superficial investigations. When she presented these figures to the vice president, his initial reaction was that the group had their priorities all wrong: they should emphasize accuracy and thoroughness rather than personal service. Eleanor, having anticipated this reaction, had prepared her case for the cost-effectiveness of personal service. She had projected the number of clients who would be offended by a rigid, intrusive style of customer relations from her staff and reminded the vice president of the highly competitive nature of the insurance business.

It was a long meeting with intense discussion. The most difficult challenge for Eleanor was to relate her concern for the well-being of her staff and excellent customer service to the vice president's concern for the bottom line. She needed to be completely clear about both her customer service values and the financial concerns of the company. She had to make a financial case for staff excellence and good customer relations. At the end of the meeting, the vice president agreed to Eleanor's request for additional staff for a one-year trial period. At the end of that period they would review the additional staff based on the department's performance in terms of client numbers, identification of problematic claims, and overall financial performance.

The Outcome Affects Related Mismatches

Eleanor's group took control of a work overload mismatch that was contributing to burnout. However, the group could not address the work overload problem without also considering issues of values and control. A clear sense of values enabled the group to choose among the many legitimate demands on their time and energy. They needed to select among those demands in a way that made sense to them; a random selection of demands would have simply increased their cynicism by suggesting that nothing really mattered. The experience of going through the process also strengthened their sense of community. The group had worked together in such a way that they had gotten to know one another better. And their communications with the larger organization gave their group a stronger identity with that organization.

The Outcome Is a Process

As a result of this process, the group gained a balance that seemed sustainable. The group was well aware that this crisis would be followed by more problems requiring further changes in the way they worked. Their main accomplishment was initiating a self-sustaining process for improving their work life, not solving all of their present and future difficulties.

To assess the impact of this intervention, Eleanor monitored her feelings and those of co-workers in the subsequent months. She attended to signs of exhaustion and cynicism in her department. The group assessed its performance in biweekly meetings, emphasizing the four customer service values as well as performance indicators such as caseloads, number of questionable cases, and average processing times.

TRYING TO ACHIEVE SOME CONTROL

Stan felt that he no longer had control over the type and quality of care he provided as a psychologist. To get some distance from his job, he took a couple weeks off to go ocean kayaking in Puget Sound. One evening, back in the cabin after a long day on the water, Stan got into a conversation with two other kayakers. He contrasted the satisfying feeling of tiredness that follows physical exertion in the fresh air with the dispirited exhaustion he felt after a week at work, where he was pushed around by a tight-fisted bureaucracy that seemed to have nothing but contempt for him and his clients. One of his companions, feeling at that moment fairly removed from the demands of the material world, asked, "Is the payoff from the company really worth it?" and Stan was left at a loss for words.

It Starts with a Person

For the remainder of his stay at the kayak camp, Stan's thoughts were haunted by that question. Upon his return to the city, he decided to take some action. First, he consulted the research on the number of psychotherapy sessions required to be effective with various forms of psychological distress. He found that the average number of sessions matched the maximum number established by his company's guidelines, but that research confirmed that a considerable proportion of people with a given problem required more than the average. He reread the ethical codes of conduct for psychologists, attending especially to the requirement of putting client needs first.

It Becomes a Group Project

Stan contacted a dozen psychologists who worked for the same managed care operation and invited them to a meeting at his house. He said that they had reached a crisis point in terms of losing control over their responsibility for patient care.

Stan started the meeting by describing his frustrations and the sense of exhaustion, cynicism, and helplessness that had dominated his feelings for the previous months. He said that what he was experiencing was burnout, pure and simple. He was on the brink of walking away from his job. He had called this meeting because it had occurred to him that his experience was probably not unique. Their work for the company did not allow many opportunities to get together and compare notes on their experience of the work; they all provided individual services at clinics all over the city and worked on a variety of schedules.

Stan's first question to the others was whether they shared his sense of being out of control; his second question was whether that experience was burning them out. Their answer to both questions was a resounding "Yes!" and the group went on to have an animated discussion about their frustrations with their work. There was general agreement that the job did not accommodate the ideals that had led them to this profession. Caring for people lost out at every turn to the corporate profit motive. Furthermore, they did not have the clout to insist upon a humane approach to psychotherapy. Every week was a deadening series of compromises.

For Stan and the others in the group, the major issue was taking control of their work as psychologists for the benefit of their clients. The primary conflict was between the value they placed on responsiveness and the value the company placed on efficiency.

The company required predictable treatment schedules: private-sector provision of health care was not manageable without predictable costs, and the primary cost was the psychologist's time. A second company value was accessibility: the health insurance plan promised customers access to a psychologist when they needed one. The company did not want to have patients waiting while all the staff was tied up with interminable cases. Long waiting lists would mean disgruntled customers who would pressure their employers to consider the services of competing managed care plans. In addition, the company projected future staffing based on a certain distribution of psychological problems that would require the availability of a specific number of psychologists. If the cost and availability of the psychologists were unpredictable, the company would not be able to fulfill its obligations within its budget.

Like the company, the psychologists too valued accessibility. They felt it was important that services be available when people needed them. The psychologists valued efficiency as well. They were aware that excessive costs brought benefits to no one—the company would either pass the costs onto the customer or replace psychologists with treatment providers who could serve clients more cheaply. Thus, the psychologists did not perceive the company's values of accessibility and efficiency to be irrelevant or damaging; the problem was a matter of emphasis.

After considerable discussion, the group agreed that imposing a fixed limit on the number of sessions supported the values of accessibility and efficiency in a way that was directly opposed to their own values of personal service and responsiveness. The task was to negotiate with the company for an enduring resolution to this value conflict.

It Connects to the Organization

Stan and the group drafted a proposal to take to the managed care company. A primary point was that the psychologists as a group would commit to an overall average number of sessions for a set of identified psychological problems. The company would give them discretion to extend the number of sessions when warranted by the specific conditions of a particular person. A group of psychologists would meet to consider cases in which their colleagues had decided to extend treatment. They would make recommendations for alternative approaches to treatment based on this review. They would also use the information they gained in this way for further negotiations with the company on guidelines for estimating the number of sessions required to address certain problems. Thus, the proposal sought a new balance between the conflicting values of accessibility/efficiency and personal service/responsiveness.

After consulting widely with other psychologists providing services, Stan's group took the proposal to the company. Management had reservations about the approach because it introduced uncertainty into costs and staffing projections. Increased control for the psychologists came at the expense of management control, and they were unsure the benefit justified the inconvenience. These two perspectives sparked a lively debate. The management perspective emphasized financial control as the critical issue while the psychologists emphasized the quality of service and a manageable work life. Management doubted that a group of independent professionals could control their individual billings. They believed that each psychologist would try to be the one who billed for more sessions. They believed that the allocation for psychological services would be spent long before the year was over and the company would have to choose between overrunning its budget or alienating customers. For the psychologists, the primary challenge was to convince management that current levels of performance could not continue because of the strain they were experiencing. Second, they had to convince management that they were capable of managing their financial concerns.

Ultimately, management was convinced by the evidence of burnout problems among the psychologists, the research that indicated the necessity of additional treatment sessions, and the psychologists' willingness to take full responsibility for meeting their treatment objectives. The two sides agreed to a one-year trial period for the new arrangement.

Once again, although the solution entailed the group's adapting to the current state of things, it also entailed communicating outside of the group to the company and asking for additional resources. The psychologists did not accept the organizational policy as something to which they had merely to adapt but as something to change.

The Outcome Affects Related Mismatches

In this case, the group addressed a mismatch in control that was contributing to burnout. However, they found that they could not address the control problem without also considering workload, rewards, and values. To take control of their work life, they eventually had to make decisions about workload and the distribution of rewards. They wanted more control over their work in order to adhere more consistently to their shared values. The experience of conducting the process also strengthened their sense of community. They learned more about one another and gained a stronger sense of their identity as a group.

The Outcome Is a Process

Once again, the outcome is an ongoing process, not a happy ending. The group gained a balance that seemed sustainable. The company accepted their proposal on a tentative basis, expressing skepticism that they could maintain collegial control over a potentially divisive issue. The group would need to develop quickly its capacity to resolve conflict among its members and between itself and the company.

Stan and his group monitored the impact of the intervention by discussing their reaction to their work. They found a greater sense of effectiveness that seemed to come as much from their participation in the intervention itself as from the impact of the new procedures. A survey of psychologists in the group provided evidence of decreased burnout on all three dimensions: exhaustion, cynicism, and ineffectiveness. In addition to monitoring burnout informally and in surveys, the group kept track of performance indicators, that is, sessions and outcomes for clients. In the course of these discussions the group identified new issues on which further discussions with the company would be based.

Six months into the new program, a psychologist who worked for the same company in another city contacted Stan to learn more about the process he had initiated. Stan was particularly pleased to learn that a manager for the company there had recommended the new procedure to this psychologist. It seemed that the managers were finding that things could operate smoothly even with less central control in the organization.

TRYING TO GAIN MORE REWARDS

John felt bitter about the lack of meaningful rewards he was given for his work as a public school teacher. The pay and benefits seemed inadequate compensation for the emotional demands of the job, the long hours required for thorough preparation, and the diverse range of relationships he had to maintain with parents, administrators, and students.

It Starts with a Person

John shared his frustration with a small group of teachers at his school. Although he was convinced that sharing his feelings was better than keeping them bottled up inside, he was also aware that the repetitive airing of anger and frustration was not doing anybody much good. It was time to move beyond that sort of gripe session.

John persuaded five other teachers to meet with him during spring break. Before that meeting, he read over documents from the teachers' union on wages and benefits. This reading confirmed what he knew—that the teachers' salaries and benefits were set in the contract for another two years. It also confirmed what he suspected—that teaching salaries and benefits were influenced more by the large supply of new graduates from teaching programs looking for work than by the demands of the job. The great number of teachers looking for work kept the salaries low. It was clear that teachers were not going to be able to change their salary in their current jobs in the short term. John was convinced that the present situation was intolerable and that teachers needed to approach the problem from a new angle.

It Becomes a Group Project

John began the meeting by laying out the conclusions of this research. He noted the disparity between teachers' salaries and those for people with comparable credentials, responsibilities, and demands in other jobs. He noted that it was impossible for the group to influence salary levels in the short run. He concluded that they had three options:

1. Leave this job for a better paying teaching job elsewhere
2. Adjust their contributions in accordance with their compensation
3. Improve the nonmaterial rewards of the job

The group agreed that this list summed up their options. They saw the first option as both unattainable and undesirable. It was unattainable because teaching salaries were fairly equal across the city while family ties argued strongly against moving elsewhere. It was undesirable because they saw their problem as a chronic one in the teaching profession and they felt responsible to address it, not merely to escape it. They set to work on the second and third options.

John defined the situation: "The job will pay a set amount of money as long as we fulfill the minimal requirements of the job. While there may be a few people in our school whose level of performance is barely above that minimum level of performance, the norm within our school is to work far above that level. To me, this means that we are working for other kinds of rewards: the experience of helping our students learn, the satisfaction of developing a new approach to a difficult topic, or the respect of our colleagues. There are real problems with the financial compensation of this job, but in addition to those, we are having problems in finding these other types of rewards."

The group discussed the rewards that they valued in their work. As John had stated, the principal rewards involved interaction with students and with the process of teaching. The respect of their colleagues was a powerful reward because fellow teachers understood the challenges of teaching and appreciated the difference between work that was truly high quality and work that merely appeared to be so. They felt that administrators, especially those from the district office, tended to be wowed by flashy technical triumphs that actually often contributed little to learning.

However, it was difficult to gain these rewards because of pressures from various directions. A big problem was the overall increase in workload and decrease in resources during the current tight financial regime. Cutbacks in support staff had teachers doing a lot of the rudimentary work around the school that would more effectively be done by teaching assistants. Cutbacks in professional support staff meant that teachers had to add managing the library to their day. The latter consequence of downsizing not only increased the teachers' workload but also diminished the library's usefulness: the teachers did not organize it or teach its use to students as well as a professional librarian would. The teachers referred to this move as "downsizing to inefficiency." As they spent more time in nonproductive chores about the school, they had less time to prepare for classes and to teach. Even collegial appreciation was rare because no one had the opportunity to find out what others were doing.

The teachers concluded that the school's values seemed to be in a muddled state. The administration spoke of the need for efficiencies in the current economic difficulties, but the actions on the front lines of teaching were making the job less efficient. Teachers were doing work that could be provided more cost-effectively by people with different training and occupations, while less thorough lesson preparation resulted in less effective teaching because it was less responsive to the specific needs of the students. The management of the school was interfering with the most powerful non-monetary reward available—recognition by respected colleagues.

John and his colleagues developed a plan in which they identified areas of activity that were consuming their time and energy but providing little value in return to either the teachers, the students, or the school's administration.

At the top of the list was technical work in the school's computer lab, which was becoming outmoded at an accelerating rate. The teachers agreed that there was little in stand-alone computer programs that made a noticeable contribution to students' learning. Most students used the computers to e-mail one another and play a variety of games that had been installed on the machines to make them user-friendly. But ample opportunities for such activities seemed available outside of school, whereas the age and design of these computers prohibited their effective use in the classroom. The plan was to stop attending to the computers: when they stopped working, that would be the end of them.

The second area they addressed was the library. They would no longer provide a stopgap for the librarian. They believed that the current system was worse than having no library at all. It was unrewarding and did not create an effective resource. The school library would remain closed until funds were found to staff it properly.

In addition to suggesting that their involvement in other non-productive activities be curtailed, the proposal called for a clear and accountable increase in high-quality teaching. The teachers would monitor this activity in a public way by providing a monthly award throughout the school term for a fine example of effective and innovative teaching. The award could go to a group of teachers collaborating on a project, a single teacher, or a classroom.

It Connects to the Organization

The group wrote up a description of the program and discussed their ideas with the other teachers in the school, incorporating their suggestions into the final version as well. The response from management was guarded. The administration found itself in a dilemma between meeting the district's regulations for technical education and library facilities on the one hand and supporting the teachers' commitment to effective teaching on the other. Pressure from parents and the political world for greater teaching effectiveness was very much on their minds. They saw the teachers' initiative as the first step in a process that would result in their running things without reference to either the school board's mandate or the pressures from concerned parents. And some in management thought that keeping up the pressure on teachers was an effective and necessary way of forcing overpaid and underproductive staff members out of the system.

This brush-off from management threw the group into disarray. Some of the teachers wanted to drop the initiative entirely. They were worried about being branded as troublemakers. Although their work life was strained, they were afraid that management could make things much worse. After considerable and heated discussion, two teachers left the group while the others put together a formal request for a meeting with the school's management group to present their case.

Prior to that meeting the teachers presented their perspective at a parent-teacher meeting. They hoped to gain the active support of this group for their proposal. This would make the issues public and remove one of the principal's concerns—potential problems with parents. Consequently, when the teachers met later with the administration management group, they were accompanied by the head of the parent-teacher association, who spoke enthusiastically about the proposal and its potential for enhancing the students' quality of education.

To avoid a direct, public confrontation with the teachers, the principal managed to find funds for a part-time person to keep the library and computer lab open a few hours a day, thus meeting the district office's minimal requirements for these services. The principal was well aware that a more meaningful solution was necessary in the long run, but for the moment the teachers' initiatives were gaining impressive publicity and momentum.

Once again, although the solution meant that the group had to adapt to circumstances it also involved taking some assertive actions, such as communicating with the school administration about a different and more cost-effective way of doing things. In turn, the district and school administrations learned that they needed to develop more insightful solutions to the school's management problems.

The Outcome Affects Related Mismatches

John's group focused on insufficient reward and its contribution to burnout. But to reach a solution, the group had to consider values, control, fairness, and workload as well. The experience of going through the process also strengthened their sense of community.

The Outcome Is a Process

Once again, the outcome is a process, not a happy ending. Once again, the group reached a new balance that seemed sustainable. The school administration accepted their proposal. It used its strained financial resources to meet the letter of the law from the school district. The principal was aware that he would have to face significant financial challenges in the year ahead now that his multitasking solution to the library and computer lab problems was gone.

John told his colleagues that the most important measure of success was the "grumble level": how often teachers grumbled in the staff room about unrewarding work. Other important measures were the quality of innovative projects recognized in the following year and the fulfillment experienced by the people who had shared in the process.

TAKING INDIVIDUAL INITIATIVE WITHIN AN ORGANIZATIONAL FRAMEWORK

The stories presented in this chapter were of three individuals who managed to find the energy and enthusiasm to address organizational shortcomings in response to a crisis experience of burnout. Eleanor, Stan, and John took leadership roles within their work groups and initiated a group process that resulted in correcting a mismatch between themselves and their jobs. They built on the power inherent in their professional expertise and their importance to the employer in meeting the organization's objectives. They all faced the difficulty of initiating change from the front lines.

An advantage they all shared was that each of them belonged to an organization that thought of itself as concerned for the well-being of both staff and clientele. For the most part, the binds in which these three people found themselves resulted from management flaws: the organization had implemented policies without thorough consultation with their staff members. It was concerned about its employees, although that concern had not taken top priority in decision making or been effectively implemented in management strategies.

Admittedly, the situation may be quite different for employees in an organization that tends to exploit those unfortunate enough to work for it. Those individuals may have to resort to more drastic and confrontational strategies to make their point. Their employment could even be threatened before things turn around in a meaningful way. The following is a case in point:

> At a manufacturing company, many of the workers were unhappy with recent changes in policy that affected rewards, workload, and fairness. The company had shifted from an hourly wage to a

piecework rate, and no longer paid extra for overtime. The result was that the workers were forced to work more for less money. A group of them tried to talk with management but were told that they could quit if they didn't like the terms of the job. Many of the workers were immigrant women supporting families, and losing their job was something they didn't want to risk. The workers then tried to organize a union but for months were subjected to various obstructive tactics, such as threats of being fired and vandalism of their property. Then the company collaborated with the Immigration and Naturalization Service in conducting a workplace raid, and over fifty workers were deported just before payday. The remaining workers walked out, and over the next few days the majority of them joined a local union. Eventually, the union was able to negotiate some better working conditions for the employees.

Although some job situations can be as bad as this, in other cases the threats are more subtle. For example, in one law firm that was undergoing "redeployment" (that is, downsizing), a human resources manager gave misleading negative feedback to some of the secretarial staff—warning them that they might be reassigned, that their futures were uncertain—and thus gently scaring them into leaving peacefully and without liability to the firm. In other organizations, implied threats consist even more of bark rather than bite, given social pressures on organizations to act responsibly toward their employees. Nevertheless, these intimidating tactics can still have a chilling effect on initiatives for change.

In these three case studies, successful resolution was achieved through a special commitment from staff members, a shared experience among colleagues, and some fortunate circumstances. This is a risky business at best. The process is more straightforward when a CEO realizes that the company needs to do better by its people— more straightforward, but also fraught with its own perils. Crisis management on the scale of an entire organization requires considerable resources. And although a particular intervention may help some employees, it can also be intrusive and disruptive for people who don't think they have a problem with burnout.

It is better for everyone involved if organizations manage themselves in a way that prevents burnout from occurring in the first place. In Chapter Six, we'll see how such prevention can be accomplished. And we'll see an additional advantage of the prevention approach: it not only reduces the risk of burnout but also enhances positive engagement with work.

6

Preventing Burnout and Building Engagement

So why wait for burnout to happen before doing something constructive about it? Why not deal with the problem when it's minor rather than major? As we argued in Chapter Four, preventing burnout is not just a noble goal to pursue—it makes economic sense. It is far better to invest in avoiding burnout than to pick up the costs in its wake. But reducing the possibility of burnout is only part of a preventive approach. Even more important is increasing the chances that people remain engaged with their work.

Focusing on engagement means focusing on the energy, involvement, and effectiveness that employees bring to a job and develop through their work. A focus on building engagement helps build more effective organizations. Successful organizations have strong cultures that are consistent with their missions. Those major corporations that compete successfully on quality make a serious commitment to their work. Excellence is not simply a slogan to use in advertisements or annual reports. A commitment to quality is evident in every aspect of such organizations. Most important, employees throughout the company must receive support for their pursuit of excellence. With motivated and skilled employees, the day-to-day issue for management is to remove barriers to effective work while the long-term issue is to develop an organizational environment that provides them with ever more effective support.

The important question is not just how to solve problems but how to create new possibilities.

In this chapter, we will focus primarily on a goal orientation rather than on simple problem solving. It's not that a problem orientation is unimportant—indeed, it's sometimes essential—but it soon runs into limits. An organization cannot anticipate and avoid every situation in which employees may feel overworked, frustrated, or unappreciated. But a goal orientation continues to evolve. It can enhance the organization's capacity to respond effectively to the strains it will inevitably encounter. The initiatives that we'll consider in this chapter go beyond day-to-day management to enhance the relationships of people with their jobs. Their ultimate goal is to build something positive, not simply to eliminate a negative.

LOOKING AT THE JOB-PERSON MISMATCH FROM THE ORGANIZATIONAL PERSPECTIVE

In this long-term view, the basic approach we advocate is taken at the organizational rather than the individual level. This approach concentrates on the conditions in the workplace rather than on the unique qualities of each person. It focuses on the structures and processes that shape life in the organization rather than on the crises encountered by employees. It requires a genuinely collaborative effort within the larger organization to identify broad-based solutions and implement them.

The organizational approach tackles the job-person mismatch from the perspective of the workplace rather than from that of the worker. Thus, it analyzes areas of organizational life. The six areas in question—workload, control, rewards, community, fairness, and values—are shaped by organizational practices and structures. Management can control these practices and structures, and therefore they are the targets of an organizational intervention. For example, management cannot directly change an employee's sense of fairness or endow that individual with a sense of control. But management

can develop practices—such as supervision skills or safety procedures—that affect the employee's sense of fairness or control. Figure 6.1 illustrates how management processes and structures affect
the six areas of organizational life and how they in turn affect engagement with work.

Thus, the goal of an organizational strategy is to build management structures and processes that promote engagement and
prevent burnout. To do this, up-to-date information is needed on
the state of the organization as far as those six areas are concerned,
on the management practices or structures that shape the six areas,
and on the state of the employees on the burnout-engagement
continuum.

FIGURE 6.1. The Connection Between Processes and Structures
and Engagement with Work.

Management Processes and Structures

Mission and goals
Central management
Supervision
Communication
Performance appraisal
Health and safety

Six Areas of Organizational Life

Workload
Control
Reward
Community
Fairness
Values

Engagement with Work

Energy
Involvement
Effectiveness

But if the job is the starting point in this approach, who gets the process rolling? As we saw in the last chapter, any person can initiate the crisis intervention process and accomplish a lot by cooperating with colleagues to address job-person mismatches. To achieve the kind of far-reaching change described in the preceding paragraphs, however, the leadership of central management is crucial. Furthermore, from our point of view it is good management that prevents burnout and builds engagement with work.

Step 1: It Starts with Management

It may seem surprising that during the current crisis in the job environment there are enlightened administrators who are seriously committed to promoting engagement and preventing burnout in their organizations. These effective executives and managers are not insulated from the pressures of increased competition in the private sector or reduced funding in the public sector; they are fully aware of those pressures, but they see promoting engagement as a way of addressing them. These people are convinced that to fulfill their responsibility as CEO or vice president or supervisor they must improve the work life of the people in their organizations. They are dedicated to building a sense of community among their employees, not just exploiting their talents and energy. In addition to being concerned about a well-functioning organization, these managers are clearly focused on reducing costs. Their sense of responsibility is both social and fiscal.

A fundamental difference between these managers and their more familiar counterparts—those with a more short-term perspective on their employees—is their vision for the organization. Managers who are committed to engagement look toward the future. Their employees are often highly skilled people whose work requires lifelong learning. The work of the organization requires initiative and judgment from front-line staff. It is too complex to be accomplished with standardized procedures: it's people who do the creative problem solving.

This combination of factors leads some CEOs—but not all, by any means—to conclude that an environment that builds engagement is essential for the organization's long-term success. These managers are willing to make a serious commitment to initiatives that will bring about engagement when they're convinced that the initiatives will make a difference. Because they have the power to set the organizational agenda, they can make this effort a priority for everyone. They can commit funds and other resources to the process, and they can bring in consultants to make it work more effectively. Furthermore, their position gives them a broad vision of the organization as a whole (rather than a view of just its constituent parts), so that they can assess the potential impact of changes in organizational policies.

Step 2: It Becomes an Organizational Project

An organizational intervention to build engagement and prevent burnout is, of necessity, an inclusive project. It is not something done *to* people, but something done *with* people. In order for the intervention to be ultimately successful, the larger organization has to buy into it. There has to be a shared vision of the purpose of the project and its ultimate value to the organization. All levels and units must be committed to being a part of the project from beginning to end. This means that various people must be given meaningful roles to play in the process and that important leaders and stakeholder groups besides central management must endorse it. And finally, there has to be a shared agreement that the outcome of the project will really have an effect on organizational policy.

Communication is essential for the success of any organizational project. The organization needs to consider the staff members' perspectives on the six areas of organizational life and the relevant management processes and structures. To gain their perspective, the organization needs more than an upward flow of information. A successful process shares information among the work units across the organization as well as up and down the hierarchical ladder. This task exceeds in scope and nature the standard communication processes of large organizations. Much of the standard information flow about people in these settings is either highly abstract and general or too specific and anecdotal.

General information about staff often misses the point—does not make the connection between people and the problems and opportunities in their work—because it presents individuals in stereotypical ways. For example, a report about what nurses think will miss the mark much of the time. There are many kinds of nursing specialties, and within each one the nurses confront unique challenges and opportunities at work. Every nurse has personal concerns and aspirations that result in a distinct relationship with work. In contrast, anecdotal information is too specific. Although a story about the successes or difficulties that one person encounters at work may be rich in the details of day-to-day life, it may represent only the concerns of a few people rather than the central issues for the organization.

People who are intent on building a better work environment need information that will help them make sense of the complex relationships employees have with their work. That information must encompass many individuals to cover the territory, but it must also be kept simple to be understandable. Administrators leading a change initiative need to understand what drives the relationships between employees and their jobs if they are to identify the strengths on which the organization can build. They need to know the hot issues for staff in order to take definitive action on critical problems. They need to know the points at which a change in management policy will bring about an improvement in organizational life. And staff members need an opportunity to express their viewpoints to management and to one another in order to understand that they matter to the organization—and are active, important contributors. For these reasons, the organizational project requires a staff survey that is well designed and thoroughly executed. (We will describe what makes a good staff survey in the following section.)

Step 3: It Connects to People

Although the project is an organizational one, it needs to have a direct relationship with people throughout the organization. Whatever their job title or organizational unit, all employees need to see how the project is relevant to what they do at work. This connection will be most clearly established if they become involved, active participants in the process. And if they have input into the organization's understanding of itself, they will be much more willing to share in the implementation of the intervention. To be most effective, the intervention has to be translated from general organizational policy into terms that are relevant for various work groups and individuals.

An organizational intervention may focus on a single area of organizational life or encompass a cluster of them. In either case, the underlying principle is to identify strategies for improving the fit between workers and the workplace. If job-person mismatches can be reduced so that people establish harmonious relationships with their work in the six areas, then the jobs they do will be enriched by greater energy, involvement, and effectiveness.

Step 4: The Outcome Affects Related Mismatches

The organizational project can target one or more mismatches for an intervention effort. Regardless of its intended outcome, the process itself is likely to affect particular areas, especially community, fairness, and values. If the process is one in which there is greater communication and collaboration between individuals and work groups (and particularly those that don't have regular contact with each other), it will increase people's mutual knowledge and understanding of one another and thus enhance their sense of community. If the process is one in which people are given a voice, issues are recognized, and conflicts resolved, then there will be a greater feeling of fairness in the workplace. And if the process focuses on organizational values and how they relate to the work people do to carry out the organizational mission, the resulting clarification of values will reduce value conflicts and their detrimental effects.

Step 5: The Outcome Is a Process

When its procedures and structures are responsive to people, an organization can foster a harmonious relationship between people and their job environment. By promoting engagement and preventing burnout, such interventions enhance the organization's capacity to pursue its mission. The result is a more harmonious organizational community—but this in itself is not a "happy ending." Rather, it is an ongoing process by which the organization can continue to adapt to ever-changing circumstances in a way that promotes engagement with work. In other words, the process of solving problems in accordance with shared organizational values is not a temporary fix. The investment in this organizational process is not only for immediate but also for long-term benefits.

FINDING OUT WHAT'S GOING ON

An effective organizational strategy to prevent burnout and build engagement begins with a staff survey on key aspects of organizational life. Just as a financial audit is a standard operating procedure to assess how an organization deals with its fiscal responsibilities, a staff audit assesses how an organization deals with its responsibilities to its employees. In other words, it reveals the extent to which the workplace is promoting their productivity and engagement.

An essential criterion for doing a staff survey is an accurate, timely, and meaningful flow of information about what is going on. With such information, the organization can use its limited resources to address the key issues more effectively. Without it, management may initiate programs that intend to help employees but completely miss the mark. The programs may be appropriate in some areas of the organization but unnecessary or even counterproductive for other work groups. In tight economic times, organizations cannot afford to waste time and energy in this way.

Thus, there are two major phases to the organizational strategy: finding out what's going on with the organization's workforce, and then using this information to improve the organizational culture. The first phase involves surveying people and then interpreting the results. Specifically, the first phase seeks to assess the following:

- The levels of burnout and engagement among staff
- The extent of job-person mismatch in the six areas of organizational life
- The relationship between the management structures and processes and the six areas

The second phase of the strategy concerns how the survey will affect the organization. The goals of this phase are to establish ongoing processes:

- To improve communication throughout the organization, both among the staff and between the staff and management
- To implement organizational changes that promote engagement with work and prevent burnout

Effective management of the entire strategy is critical to the success of any subsequent change. Also critical is active participation of all the employees and management in all aspects of the process: preparation, implementation, interpretation, and application.

GETTING OFF TO A GOOD START

Building commitment from employees to participate in the staff survey often comes down to a commitment from management to use its results to shape policy. Central management shows this commitment when it takes certain actions:

- Defines clear objectives for the staff survey

- Establishes a work group with members from across the organization to manage the design and implementation of the survey

- Develops a plan for communicating and working with survey results

- Establishes task forces to address central issues emerging from the survey and develop proposals for change

- Develops a process for implementing these proposals

What's necessary here is thoughtful planning before doing the actual survey. Such planning not only establishes organizational commitment but also makes the entire process more efficient and effective. Organizations often lose momentum if they wait until after the arrival of a survey report to begin planning how to use the information and to assign people to take responsibility for the various findings. By the time things are in place, many staff members may lose interest in the survey or its results may be overshadowed by subsequent events. If there is a clear plan concerning the use of survey findings from the outset, then the relevance and timeliness of the survey will be increased.

Asking the Right Questions

We have used survey methods extensively in our research on burnout. Our work with managers in many different kinds of organizations has led to the development of our own Staff Survey, which supplements our burnout measure with complete information on the six areas of job-person mismatch. The Staff Survey is designed to be a practical source of information for people determined to build engagement with work. Our experience has confirmed its usefulness.

As part of the survey, the burnout measure—the Maslach Burnout Inventory, or MBI—assesses each individual's experience on the continuum from burnout to engagement with work. Other questions assess staff members' perceptions of the six areas of organizational life, that is, workload, control, reward, community, fairness, and values. The Staff Survey also looks beyond these six areas to assess relevant management structures and processes, offering distinct measures of direct supervision and distant management, communication networks, health and safety concerns, performance appraisal systems, and the performance of work groups. The survey provides information on the current state of inclusive decision-making practices, the relationship between departmental decision-making procedures and employees' sense of control in their work, and the relationship between control and employees' energy, involvement, and effectiveness. Taken together, this information indicates the current state of affairs in regard to decision making and the potential for changes in decision-making policies to have an impact on employees across major sectors of the organization. (See the Appendix for more information on the Staff Survey and the Maslach Burnout Inventory.)

In addition to these basic measures, the survey may also need some customized questions to assess unique circumstances that are relevant to the six areas of organizational life. Different organizations espouse very different kinds of values. The best way to develop customized questions is to use focus groups to gather relevant material. The focus groups need not include everyone in the organization, but it is important that they represent every functional work group in every area. The task of these focus groups is to generate a comprehensive list of the organizational factors that relate to these six areas. Thus they identify critical factors influencing workload, control, reward, community, fairness, and values. For organizations with little experience in conducting focus groups, it may be necessary to bring in an outside consultant. The information generated by the focus group process is incorporated into questions on the survey.

Getting the Right Answers

An important issue in conducting the survey is making sure that as many people as possible answer it. If the survey is to be at all useful, it must reflect the experiences and opinions of everyone—not just particular subgroups, not just the people who are doing fine, but the full range of employees. A well-planned survey process makes time for people to participate, emphatically ensures their confidentiality, and makes a firm commitment to using the results. Scheduling time to complete the survey, as well as providing coverage when necessary to free up the staff, is a basic management job. Using an external survey consultant can increase staff members' confidence in the confidentiality of their responses.

Analyzing the Findings

When the survey results are analyzed, the responses should be associated with subsections of a large organization. This is done because people in different organizational units differ in their concerns in a way that requires distinct interventions. Service providers confront opportunities and challenges that are quite different from those of support staff; front-line staff and middle management have different concerns as well. The survey asks questions in a way that pertains to the work of anyone in the organization in order to establish a common point of reference, but it analyzes the responses in a way that promotes action appropriate to the needs of a specific sector of the organization.

Getting Some Useful Results

Once the survey has been conducted and the information analyzed, a report should be written about the results. A useful survey report provides a concise summary of the findings in a manner that is readable and thought provoking for everyone, and it clearly addresses the objectives of a staff audit. It indicates the state of the overall community while providing information on the specific mismatches staff members encounter in their work.

The report stage is critical to the success of the intervention. Many employee survey projects stumble at this stage because they miss the basic point of the report, which is to help the organization find solutions to its problems. Some of these reports are huge, containing endless pages of frequency tables, flooding people with data and technical jargon. But the organization does not need tons of data. Rather, it needs answers to specific questions. For a report to be useful, it must be short and to the point and must address the objectives of the survey. To achieve this end, the group conducting the survey must be skilled and have a plan to conduct insightful analyses. If an analysis is to be informative, there must be a deep understanding of a large and complex set of information and a thorough plan for both the analysis and the reporting.

After the survey project is completed, the organization can pursue several strategies for discussing the results and using them to guide interventions. One such strategy is to give each work group in the organization information about its profile compared with that of the larger organization. This information serves as a point of comparison for survey issues. For example, is burnout prevalent in some units but nonexistent in others? Does one work group have a major problem with value conflicts while another reports concerns about workload and rewards? Such comparative information also provides a basis for determining the relationship between the work group and the organization, whether it is in harmony with the organizational mission or in conflict with it.

Another strategy is to identify some of the key issues that have emerged from the survey results and then establish a strategic task force to develop initiatives for each one. For example, one particular unit within the organization may be facing a unique situation with regard to community and fairness issues, and a task force could be set up to deal with just that. Or perhaps there is a control issue throughout the organization; in that case, a more broad-based task force would be required to generate some companywide solutions.

In all cases, these task forces consider alternative proposals for dealing with these problems and make recommendations to the larger organization. Again, like the focus groups through which survey questions are developed, these task forces must have a membership that is broadly representative of the units or organizational levels they are addressing. If any of their subsequent recommendations is going to be embraced and implemented by people in the organization, those people need to feel that they had some say in what that recommendation is.

A third organizational strategy may be necessary to resolve conflict. The survey process may bring into the open conflicts that have been present for some time and that interfere with employees' capacity to feel engaged with their work. Some conflicts are among people within a work group, others are between two groups or between a group and the larger organization. Establishing effective processes for conflict resolution is an important goal for any organization, and achieving it will greatly enhance the sense of community and fairness.

IMPROVING THE ORGANIZATIONAL CULTURE: A CASE STUDY

Thus, the process of building engagement with work starts with a management plan and works through collaborative projects in key sectors of organizational life. The intervention focuses primarily on a management structure or practice that influences one or more of the six areas in which person-job mismatches occur. The survey identifies issues with the greatest potential for influencing staff members' engagement with work. Task forces develop initiatives to promote change in these areas.

So far, so good. But actually the most difficult part of the process is yet to come. Implementation of the change is the most difficult because the expectations for its success are often not realistic. Organizational interventions take time. Their goal is much more ambitious than addressing a specific source of strain or frustration for a few people. Their goal is to change practices and structures that influence the work life of people throughout the organization. These changes are not only more difficult to implement but also more difficult to evaluate. Organizational initiatives are never an instant success with everyone—their success builds over time. At first, the demands of doing things in a new way may well outweigh the benefits of an innovation. As people develop the necessary skills and expectations, the benefits become more obvious. Part of managing an intervention is keeping the process going during this transition. Organizational interventions also require broad-based assessments to determine their impact on the management structure or practice they target as well as staff members' consequent engagement with work.

So what does an actual organizational intervention process look like? And what actions are taken to prevent burnout and promote engagement? Let's take an extended look at a case study of a hospital, and see how the process we've just described unfolds in that setting.

It Starts with Management

David Molloy, the CEO of Metropolitan Hospital, became dedicated to engagement-oriented management through his experience as a family physician and as a manager. As a family physician, he developed an appreciation for the complex demands the modern world makes on people at work and at home. As a manager, he had confidence in the expertise and dedication of people with whom he worked but also reservations about the extent to which health care organizations could support staff efforts. In his previous job as vice president of medicine at another hospital, Molloy had applied quality management practices to medicine.

The board of Metropolitan Hospital—which was a 750-bed hospital with a full-time staff of thirty-five hundred and a part-time staff of five hundred—anticipated that, over the next five years, the hospital would face the most significant challenge to its survival since it began providing health care to the community a century ago. The current state government was nearing the end of a term of office that had been characterized by labor unrest, stagnant private sector development, and political scandal. The government had been fairly generous to the hospital, but this demonstration of concern for the people was not enough to offset the damage done by its poor overall political performance over the previous four years. The opposing party was thus nearly certain to win, and it championed small government, fiscal responsibility, and, specifically, reduced state involvement in health care. The common wisdom was that Metropolitan Hospital would go through a significant downsizing and that it would go through it soon.

The board appointed David Molloy as CEO to further its goal of promoting participatory management in what had been a highly centralized organization. Molloy's predecessor had ruled the hospital in an autocratic manner through two management committees, one at each of the hospital's two sites. The board anticipated that this structure and management style were not appropriate to the dynamic economic and political environment of public sector health care in the 1990s. It concluded that active community support would be critical to the institution's survival and that quality of patient care would be critical to maintaining community support. It was also insistent that whatever new policies Molloy developed reduce the cost of running the hospital. There would be no expensive quality-of-work-life programs, and workload was nearly certain to increase as staff levels dropped with the operating budget. Further, the demands of jobs throughout the hospital were expected to grow as the hospital reduced patient numbers to focus on the most critically ill and shortened the number of days the patients remained in hospital to recuperate after a procedure.

Thus, Molloy began his term with a clear mandate from the board to develop a leaner, flexible management structure that would emphasize quality. His approach had three primary components: (1) to integrate the management of the two sites into a single management team, (2) to develop the capacity of front-line work groups to manage their part of the hospital, and (3) to enhance staff members' engagement with work, especially their involvement in high-quality health care, throughout the hospital.

It Becomes an Organizational Project

For Metropolitan Hospital, a management initiative calling for widespread participation from staff members was something new and unusual. For most it was a welcome break with tradition, but in many quarters it was viewed with suspicion. Middle management in particular was concerned with job security in a scenario that had as one of its goals a reduction in the number of management positions. Middle managers were anxious as well about potential demands from front-line hospital units newly given greater powers. Front-line supervisors did not have basic management skills because these activities were outside of their experience. They did not know how to read a balance sheet because they had not managed their budgets, and the hospital's financial information system was not designed to provide clear, timely, and well-organized information to unit heads. Betty Fitzgerald, the new vice president of patient care and the manager of all eighteen hundred nurses, was given the job of helping the nurses rise to the occasion. She knew that the hospital had a long way to go on the road to empowerment of staff through decentralization.

It Connects to People

Molloy's management team established task forces on quality management and human resource management. These two task forces had a diverse membership from throughout the two sites of the hospital. The quality management task force was led by Julia Crosby, whose background in program evaluation and organizational development had sharpened her awareness of difficulties in assessing quality services. The director of human resources, Fred Thornhill, headed the human resource task force, which included representatives from diverse professional groups: a nurse, a technologist, a physician, as well as managers. Molloy attended meetings of both groups.

The two groups' initial task was to develop a plan for promoting quality and identifying human resource issues of concern among staff members. In his discussions of this planning process with the two committees, Molloy described how a staff survey might make a good contribution to the effort. After further discussion within the task forces, the management team established a survey committee to organize a staff survey. The focus of the survey was to assess the staff's commitment to providing high-quality services. It asked staff members to identify what helped or hindered them in their pursuit of this goal.

The Outcome Affects Related Mismatches

The Metropolitan Hospital survey identified potential for improvement in all six areas of organizational life. Through a series of task forces, the hospital initiated collaborative efforts to change management structures and practices so that they would become more supportive of staff members in all six areas.

Workload. The survey results indicated a strong relationship between workload and exhaustion, which was not surprising since the hospital was experiencing increasing demand from patients and physicians for services while its funding was diminishing. In addition, responses to an open-ended survey question made it apparent that many nurses were concerned about the hospital's computer-based workload system. They felt that the system devalued those aspects of their work that it neglected to measure. For example, they believed that the system did not adequately consider the nurse's role in patient education or in emotional support, while it emphasized defined nursing procedures. Furthermore, the nurses cast doubts on the system's validity by reporting that it was common practice to make up data at the end of a busy day with more attention to what would make the ward look good than to accuracy. In sum, the nurses' concern with their workload was not so much the amount of it but rather how it was acknowledged and valued by the organization.

Fitzgerald, the manager of the nurses, established a task force to study the nursing workload system. It requested more detailed analysis of the concerns raised by the survey, noting that a range of units expressed these concerns across the hospital sites. It interviewed nurses in those units and examined data generated by the system over the previous year. A range of perspectives on the system was revealed, with some people arguing that the system did indeed give adequate consideration to education and support because it assumed that they were an integral part of effective nursing rather than identifying them as distinct services. But others argued that the hospital required an entirely new approach to workload measurement. Over the following year, the task force worked with the company that marketed the system to modify the program (the company was motivated to undertake this revision because similar issues had been raised elsewhere).

By the time the task force had fulfilled its mandate, it had made some changes in the workload system that addressed the concerns of many, but not all, staff members. For example, the system's response forms now offered a place to indicate when a patient required more support or instruction than expected for a patient with a given diagnosis.

The intervention had a profound but indirect impact on workload. First, it fostered confidence in the system among many nurses. Their confidence directly affected their engagement with work, including their energy, involvement, and effectiveness. But they still worked hard, in keeping with the hospital's determination to increase quality of services in the context of increasing demand and reduced resources.

Second, the system provided a means for recognizing instances in which the nursing staff made extraordinary efforts for demanding cases. Nurse managers began to focus on such cases in training and orientation sessions. This practice identified the extra effort of attentive patient care as a valued service of the hospital.

Third, increased recognition of support and instruction in the workload monitoring system influenced the units' staffing levels. The redistribution was not striking or sudden, but when an additional nurse was moved to a unit it had a clear impact on that unit's morale and its capacity to manage its demands.

Finally, staff members throughout the hospital deepened their understanding of the issue. They recognized the impact of the system on both the nurses' feelings about their work and the hospital's capacity to do its job. On both counts, reviewing the system was time well spent.

Control. Although they communicated a high degree of support for their front-line supervisors and nurse managers, staff members indicated reservations about the extent to which units followed inclusive decision-making procedures. They had even greater concerns about the extent to which decisions made within their work groups had an impact on the larger organization. They perceived middle management as a barrier between front-line units, which were avidly seeking empowerment, and central management, which was promoting a philosophy of inclusive decision making. Staff members were frustrated by the contrast between their heightened expectations for controlling their work and the shortcomings of the organizational procedures that would give them that control.

Wayne Sartelli, an organizational development manager in the human resource office, headed a task force on organizational decision making that requested further analysis of survey data to determine the commitment of staff at various levels to inclusive decision making. As a result, the team contrasted the degree of commitment at the various organizational levels and examined the issues that related to these groups' commitment. The results were consistent with the staff perception that issues became lost in middle management. Middle managers were both concerned about the potential disruptive impact of more proactive front-line units and dubious about the sincerity of senior management's support.

Sartelli's task force recommended a major training initiative to build middle managers' capacity to develop consensus among unit heads. The program encouraged them to initiate programs within their areas of responsibility so that initiatives from units could be put into effect with minimal delay. Sally Ingraham, a nurse manager on the task force, argued that the program should promote ideas requiring broader institutional support to central management. She had seen the demise of too many initiatives developed among her fellow intensive care managers. It seemed to her that as soon as a proposal met with any degree of opposition from above, the nurse managers dropped the idea. She believed that stubbornness was an essential quality for initiating organizational change.

The administrative reorganization of the hospital broadened the application of Ingraham's proposal. When the program got started it included both nurse managers and managers from other professional groups. The survey report clarified the extent to which managers across the hospital shared the same concerns. It also opened the way for an in-depth consideration of leadership, including a 360-degree feedback program in which managers received feedback from the people they supervised, their fellow managers, and those to whom they reported. This process made the managers more confident that they could contribute to the hospital by providing proactive leadership.

Reward. Management was surprised by a critical assessment of its performance evaluation system. Many staff members reported that they had never been given an evaluation during their many years of employment at the hospital. Of those who had recently participated in one, few found it to be of value. Responses to open-ended questions indicated that the process more often led to a regimented, superficial view of an employee's conduct rather than an appreciation of effort and expertise.

Management sought confirmation of the survey results in a frank and open discussion during a meeting of department heads. This discussion confirmed the survey's assessment of performance evaluations as rare events of little consequence.

Molloy asked Julia Crosby, head of the quality management task force, to form a performance evaluation group to redesign the content and process of performance evaluation over the coming year. This task force's eventual report to central management led to a major revamping of the system. Staff members were now permitted to provide more in-depth consideration of their contribution to the hospital. In addition, recognition and reward played more central roles in the new system. The results of the new performance appraisal system determined pay increases in the compensation plan developed under a recent union contract.

Community. The survey found severe criticisms of the organization's communication system. Many staff members, especially those in clinical units, seemed to have greater confidence in the quality and timeliness of the information in the rumor mill than in that provided in the organization's official in-house publications.

Wanda Minkowsky, the information services director, established a task force to communicate survey results. This task force made an extensive analysis of hospital communication strategies including e-mail, print media, and in-house television reports. It met with staff in units that were especially critical of the quality and timeliness of the official information flow as well as with staff who rated it quite positively. One issue that emerged was a differentiation between content and reporting: some staff members were upset with the amount of bad news that was being communicated rather than with the manner in which it was communicated. There was also the matter of trust. Many staff members did not believe that central management was not completely informed about governmental policies affecting funding or labor relations issues in the hospital; here, Wanda herself came in for direct and personal criticism. Others believed that management was as poorly informed as the staff was, and this was a matter of considerable anxiety for them.

The communications task force developed a series of recommendations concerning the format in which news was shared (open meetings, electronic media, print), the timeliness of information, and the people who played an active role in organizing the communications. They invited informal opinion leaders among the staff to contribute regularly to the hospital's newsletter on a range of topics central to the organizational culture. The intent of these recommendations was to build a stronger sense of community in the hospital. A stronger sense of community directly supports involvement and effectiveness, two characteristics of engagement with work.

Fairness. The survey also found strong criticism of the hospital's slow response to legislation for equal pay. Gender parity issues were an important issue in this large institution that had a high number of highly skilled female staff members. Respondents criticized both management for delaying the financial settlements and unions for prolonging the negotiating process through protracted bargaining. The negotiating process had generated considerable conflict among professional groups, which had each argued for the relative value of their group over others. The prolonged negotiations delayed resolution of the issue and created instead an atmosphere of resentment and competition.

Hospital management saw this survey finding as an impetus to settle the pay equity issue. Within a week of the distribution of the survey report, management reached an agreement with all the unions in question on the pay equity package for the hospital. The reduction in strife freed up more energy for work and laid a foundation for greater involvement in meaningful work.

Values. The survey provided a broad overview of the hospital's primary values. A values clarification process led prior to the survey by hospital chaplain Paul Ramos had identified four values to which staff members throughout the hospital were committed: high-quality patient care, open and honest communication, respect among people, and lifelong learning. The survey also indicated that when staff members found their work meaningful—when it allowed them to provide quality care and contributed to their professional development—they had a stronger sense of involvement and a greater sense of effectiveness. Staff members who perceived their work as being in conflict with these central values were more likely to report feelings of exhaustion and cynicism. Throughout the survey there were further indications of the relationship between strong work values and engagement with work.

The task force on organizational values integrated the survey results on values into its development of a hospital planning document. That document served as a reference point for assessing the development of core activity areas and objectives for the hospital. In many ways a wide consensus on central organizational values provides a foundation for balancing the other five job-person mismatches. Knowing what is important to an organization provides direction in addressing problems in workload, control, reward, community, and fairness.

The Outcome Is a Process

Together, these interventions constituted a range of organizational initiatives that covered all six areas in which job-person mismatches may occur. The information from the survey identified issues of concern to the organization and suggested procedures and structures through which management could enhance the quality of work life. The survey did not indicate widespread burnout throughout the hospital, although some areas reported high levels of exhaustion, cynicism, or ineffectiveness. The point of the intervention process was not to solve a current burnout problem but to enhance the quality of organizational life and prevent burnout in the future. That is, the survey did not focus on identifying undiscovered problems but rather on identifying opportunities for management to develop direct and verifiable links with the emotional and cognitive states that people experience at work.

To some extent the process of conducting the survey and distributing the report itself enhanced the sense of community in the hospital and indicated commitment to the organization's central values: high-quality patient care, open and honest communication, respect, and lifelong learning. In most instances, a task force was given a specific mandate to develop an action plan to address an issue identified in the survey. These initiatives had mixed outcomes: some were entirely successful, others were delayed by unforeseen events. The survey made a direct contribution to the resolution of the pay equity issue that was within the domain of labor negotiation. It provided information outside of the standard adversarial labor negotiations from the perspective of the organization's values, putting pressure on both management and the unions to resolve the problem.

A year and a half after the survey was completed, Metropolitan Hospital was forced into a merger with another large hospital in the city, leading to further disruptions in management structures and the day-to-day work of the staff. The hospital's progress toward engagement with work and its experience with collaborative approaches to shared problems helped it manage that transition but it did not isolate it from a turbulent environment. Instead, thanks to its experience, the hospital had developed its capacity to thrive under crisis conditions.

LESSONS LEARNED

Our argument in this chapter has been that organizational strategies that develop harmony between workers and their work are key to preventing burnout. If done right, burnout prevention is an integral part of good management.

In Chapter Five, we saw how individuals in collaboration with others in their work groups can take charge of the problems that are contributing to burnout. These crisis interventions can be effective, but they depend heavily on the insight, energy, assertiveness, and patience of key people throughout the organization. In contrast, an organizational intervention with leadership from central management is broader in scope and more likely to have an effect. This kind of intervention may take longer to implement, and it requires the collaboration of more people, but its impact is more far-reaching. In the long run, it will affect a wider range of employees. Even more important, its focus on building engagement will have a direct impact on the organization's capacity to pursue its mission. An organization that actively promotes engagement among its staff is a more effective organization.

At Metropolitan Hospital evidence of this relationship was revealed through another survey, a patient satisfaction survey that was conducted by a consulting group around the same time as the staff survey project. An analysis of both surveys found that patients were more satisfied with the hospital's services and their contacts with the staff in those units where staff were engaged with their work than in units where staff reported high levels of exhaustion and cynicism. Patients notice what staff are experiencing and it matters to them.

The twin goals of preventing burnout and building engagement are possible and necessary in today's working world. These goals cannot be easily achieved by an individual. Rather, people have to work together to make them happen. And if we all commit ourselves to the long-term process of organizational progress, we will be rewarded with workplaces that are more productive and resilient as well as more humane.

7

Promoting Human Values

In today's workplace, economic values are the primary driving force, and all else is subsidiary. Although this emphasis on economic values affects people, human concerns will not be addressed directly unless they have economic consequences. No attention will be paid to conflicts on the job, or work overload, or other job-person mismatches until their link to increased costs or lowered profits is understood. Therefore, to stress the necessity of doing something about burnout, the standard method is to provide the necessary economic translation and show how costly burnout can be—and that is indeed the argument we made in Chapter 4.

But now we want to make a different argument: that human values in and of themselves should have a high priority in the workplace. Not because of the economic consequences, not because of the public relations benefit of sounding good, but because giving priority to human values is the right thing to do. Our entire society—with all the moral principles it holds so dear—rests on a foundation of valuing people and what they can achieve. Whether freedom, family, or the pursuit of happiness or peace, these social values presume that the greatest good will come when people can use their uniquely human qualities in the service of themselves and others. This core belief in the value of humanity should be as fundamental in the workplace as it is in the home and the community.

But there is another reason to argue for human values—and that is that they make sense. A key reason people establish relationships with organizations is to accomplish something of importance. The synergy that occurs between their personal values and the organizational values that attracted them to that workplace can be a powerful driving force on the job. It is a source of creative energy that encourages groups and entire organizations to make extraordinary contributions and permits people from diverse cultural, political, and economic backgrounds to work together. Moreover, a corporation justifies its existence in a community by contributing to the overall quality of life there, not only to its economic welfare. This kind of value-added contribution is essential if an organization is to thrive in the long run.

So in this chapter we are going to take the moral high ground rather than simply rely on the lower economic one. It's not that we don't think economic values are important—clearly, they are—but rather that we think human values are equally important. And we think that importance needs to be made clear, in a way that goes beyond the standard lip service.

In our opinion, the best way to make this case is to show how a focus on human values can make a difference in the workplace. This means going beyond abstract statements to concrete actions. And once again, this means looking at the process by which an organization and its individual members figure out what their shared values are and how they are put into practice. So this chapter will focus on a process of values clarification. It will illustrate the steps to take in the process by way of the remaining three case studies we introduced in Chapter One: Martha, the hospital lab technologist (who was experiencing breakdown of community); Bill, the university network manager (absence of fairness); and Steve, the bank loan officer (value conflict).

VALUES IN THE WORKPLACE

When people think about values, they usually think about them in a positive way. After all, values are ideals we cherish and esteem, ends we strive to achieve. Our values influence our behavior in a good way, because they provide both direction and meaning to what we do on the job. Clear organizational values are a vital resource because they prevent burnout by reducing the likelihood of the six job-person mismatches we have considered throughout this book. If people are working in harmony with their values and their capabilities, then they will be more fully engaged with their work and thus less prone to burnout.

But when values are unclear or unrecognized, the resulting void means there is no positive guidance, and it can even have a negative effect on the organization. In some cases, the problem is that people have never given serious thought to what is important in their work. In other cases, things may have changed so much around the organization during the current crisis that people need to rethink their values to deal with the new problems they are encountering. Still other organizations are fragmented; individuals and groups go in different directions, working in accordance with values that are at odds with one another. In many cases, conflicting values affect day-to-day performance. The conflict may be between personal and organizational values, as when workers have to choose between excelling in their careers and spending time with their families. Or there may be a conflict between organizational values, as when a teacher has to decide whether to spend more time with students who are having difficulty in class or with gifted students who have the potential to learn more quickly than their peers. When they are both intense and difficult to resolve, all of these problems contribute to burnout.

Guiding Values

Workplace values often appear most explicitly at the top of the organization, embodied in corporate slogans or mission statements. A corporate slogan is usually a short, catchy phrase, such as "Progress is our most important product" or "We bring good things to light" or "Real-world solutions for the work you do." These slogans state to the outside world the goal of the organization and help define the organization in relation to its competition. In contrast, a mission statement is directed more to the members of the organization than to the general public, and so it is a declaration of the organization's guiding principles for achieving its goal. It confirms to the staff that their work contributes to something meaningful, enduring, and significant.

A mission statement is clearly a step in the right direction, but merely having one is not enough. The critical next step is actually carrying out these central organizational values. A mission statement is not designed to do that, for the following reasons:

- It does not address how values are used to select and implement strategies for pursuing the mission.
- It does not state how to resolve value conflicts.
- It does not acknowledge the diversity of values that may exist at the individual and work group level within a large, complex organization.

In other words, a mission statement does not provide the mechanisms for translating the expressed organizational values into the daily actions of the employees. Yet for these values to be truly meaningful, the organization has to figure out ways to convert these words into deeds.

Discrepancies Between Values and Actions

The values of an organization may become removed from its day-to-day operations for two basic reasons: it can't stick to its values or it won't. During the current crisis in the work environment, some organizations have lost the control necessary to pursue their mission effectively. Reduced government operating funds override long-term planning strategies in public sector institutions. In the private sector, organizations act contrary to their long-term aspirations in response to short-term financial pressures. The senior management responsible for implementing the strategic plan may lack the necessary resources and control.

The second group of organizations are those for which the mission statement serves a public relations function, not a strategic one. That is, the organization is not truly committed to the ideals it espouses. In this case, employees become cynical and bitter at what they see as hypocrisy on the part of management, and they may even feel betrayed by the organization.

To some extent these conflicts in value reflect different points of view within large organizations. Senior managers attend to those economic and policy developments that threaten the organization's growth or very survival. Front-line employees have more immediate concerns with the quality of the product, availability of essential services, or customer satisfaction. In the long run, these perspectives complement and support each other. The survival and economic well-being of an organization enhances its capacity to do first-rate work, while a reputation for high-quality, readily available products or services contributes to organizational survival and economic well-being. But in the short run, these two perspectives often conflict. People on each side of the issue believe the others are neglecting the larger good in favor of quick fixes while they themselves are working for the larger good.

When there is a discrepancy between values and actions, the organization will soon encounter problems in all six areas of mismatch. For example, if we look at the organizations in the three case studies discussed in this chapter, we will find that they have fine mission statements and lists of supporting objectives. Their problems arose not because they were ignoring their mission and values, but because their values were not guiding the day-to-day work.

• In the hospital lab where Martha worked, the problem was that the organization's values were not guiding the lab manager in his job. He lacked both the skills and the motivation to put into effect the organizational value of inclusive management. The problem was also with the management system, in that the hospital did not ensure that the lab manager develop skills and attitudes consistent with its values.

• In the university where Bill worked, the problem was that personnel policies were inconsistent with the value placed on expertise. Bill, as network manager, was not allowed to do the job he was hired to do and was both unfairly blamed and unfairly rewarded.

• In the bank where Steve worked, the problem was a conflict between two values, both of which were consistent with the bank's mission. With no means for resolving this conflict, Steve, as loan officer, found it difficult to maintain a workable balance between the competing objectives.

All three of these situations require more than what can be provided by an organizational mission. A more extensive process is needed for identifying values at different levels of the organization and for linking values to job behaviors.

Clarifying Organizational Values

Values clarification is a process by which an organization says what it thinks is important. It is a process through which members of the organization express their personal values, the shared values of their work group, and the values endorsed by the whole organization. It is a process through which the relationship between these three sets of values, as well as the link between values and actions, is assessed. It is a process of thorough involvement by both management and staff—rather than management alone—that examines a wide range of the organization's activities and perspectives.

This process of clarifying organizational values has several goals:

To identify the central values unifying an organization. What are the key values that are shared by all organizational members and thus make up the core of the organizational culture?

To identify the range of work group cultures within the organization. What are the different units that contribute in diverse ways to the organization's overall mission, and what are the distinct values associated with each of them?

To identify how specific values can be carried out within the organization. What is the range of actions that employees are authorized to take, and which among these are most important?

To identify values that guide means as well as ends. Here the question is not so much what goals the organization wants to achieve as which principles guide how the organization conducts its business in the pursuit of its goals.

To develop a means of resolving ongoing value conflicts within the organization. Which values are more important and take priority over others?

A PROCESS FOR CLARIFYING VALUES

So how does an organization address these issues? Basically, a values clarification process is a dialogue that is managed by an organizational task force. In a large organization this task force includes people from many diverse locations and occupations. It includes strong representation from both central management and production or service staff. The task force is responsible for initiating the process, maintaining momentum, communicating findings, and integrating changes into the organization. As you may have guessed, the process of values clarification can easily be incorporated into the organizational strategy that we described in Chapter Six.

Initiating the Process

Central management announces that the organization is embarking on a values clarification process, perhaps as part of the staff survey (we described the survey in Chapter Six). The very announce-ment of this initiative is testimony to management's commitment to use the values to guide the organization.

The process begins with focus groups, much like those described in Chapter Six. Again, these groups should be representative of the various organizational units. Using an open-ended format, focus group participants generate a comprehensive list of the values that influence their work, including the values that they bring from their personal lives, the values that provide direction for the work groups represented at the meeting, and the values of the larger organiza-tion. The focus groups should also consider the values that are com-municated publicly as well as those that are only apparent upon close examination of organizational actions.

If the organization has had little experience in developing a mission or discussing values, it's best to start with examples of val-ues relevant to the work of the organization—for example, cus-tomer service, product manufacturing, efficiency, acquisition of wealth. Consultants, either from the organization's staff or from ex-ternal agencies, can help companies with little experience to con-duct focus groups and process the information that they provide.

During this phase of the process, each focus group produces a list of values, defining them concisely and providing examples of how each plays a role in the organization. The task force then integrates the reports from all the focus groups, distilling them into a succinct, consolidated list of organizational values. Here is an example:

Martha participated in a focus group composed of people from various hospital departments and wards. The group identified col-legiality as something that the staff valued in their work and that furthered the hospital's effectiveness. In their discussions, they agreed that collegiality is a complex value based on open and honest communication and respect for others. The group rec-ommended that the values assessments section of the staff sur-vey include questions measuring respect among colleagues, collegiality, and open and honest communication.

Maintaining the Momentum

The list generated from the focus group process is incorporated into the staff survey, which is conducted with members throughout the organization. People are asked to indicate how much they personally approve of each value listed, how committed they think the organization is to it, and how difficult it is to translate it into action. They are also asked to describe the value in their own words, and to tell a brief story about an actual incident that is relevant to that value.

This process provides information about the relative emphases put on these values by the various sectors of the organization and the extent to which employees perceive the organization emphasizes one value over others. It also gives a good picture of how people see these values as influencing (or not influencing) the daily work of the organization. Here's an example:

> In their responses to the survey the bank conducted, Steve and his colleagues expressed their difficulties in dealing with the conflict between the organizational values of maximizing cash flow and providing excellent customer service. In the section on customer service, they indicated the relative importance of being responsive to customers compared with other values, such as being efficient, personalizing the service, and being prompt. When Steve was asked to put into his own words what the bank considered to be good customer service, he wrote, "We satisfy customers' needs by determining what we think is best for them." The story he told illustrated what he perceived as the bank's conflicting values, describing an incident in which an elderly couple was persuaded to sign up for a more comprehensive, full-service bank account that included many services they didn't need and that was more expensive.

Communicating the Findings

Each work group in the organization receives information about its own values and how they relate to those of the larger organization. This information is part of the staff survey report process, during which each unit is given a complete profile of its own survey results as well as a total organizational profile. This information serves as a basis for discussing work group values and relating them to the larger organization's values. Some critical issues include the following:

- Do the values of the work group differ from the organizational priorities?
- Are there points of direct conflict between the values of the work group and those of the organization?
- Are there points of direct conflict between the values of the overall work group and those of individual staff members?
- Are the values relevant to the work group's strategies as well as to its objectives? In other words, are the group's values a matter of process as well as of goals?

On the basis of this type of analysis and discussion, each work group can develop its own statement of values. This process was especially important in Bill's unit, for example, because he and his colleagues had not figured out how to accomplish their technological work in a way that was recognized and valued by the university.

Integrating Changes into the Organization

In the final phase the core group considers the reports from work groups throughout the organization. Its work at this phase has the following objectives:

To produce a concise statement of values for which there is a clear organizational consensus. This statement is a descriptive summary of the values, not simply a list. It indicates each value's relationship to the organization's mission, and the organization's primary strategy for pursuing each one.

To prepare a report about value differences or conflicts within the organization as well as any difficulties in translating values into actions. In addition to identifying and discussing these problem areas, the report could make recommendations for their solution.

Armed with this information, central management can follow through on its commitment to use the values to improve the organization. For example, a values clarification process inevitably identifies conflicts that reflect perspectives of people with a range of approaches to work, its challenges and its limitations. These conflicts can interfere with the capacity of organizations to pursue their mission as people try to resolve conflicts or to improve their position in a competitive environment. Thus a key task for management is to establish processes for conflict resolution. This might involve more informal discussion or more formal mediation, with some approaches targeting an individual and others a group. Here is where a clearly articulated mission statement can be a unifying force, providing a reference point for resolving conflicts. After all, the justification of personal or work group values is their contribution to the mission.

PUTTING VALUES TO USE

A values clarification process is a far-reaching event in the life of an organization. It is also a practical step to take. It guides actions that reduce the mismatches that lead to burnout. It contributes in a significant way to building the necessary harmony that makes engagement with work a possibility. Let's see how this process worked in our three case studies.

Building Community

Martha, the laboratory technologist, had experienced a breakdown in community. The problems involved the manager's relationships with staff and the relationships among staff members. People were not cooperating in a manner that built their effectiveness. Instead, criticism and conflict were depleting their energy and making them feel cynical about the lab's contribution to the well-being of their patients and the work of the hospital.

What values were apparent in this work setting? The manager's actions indicated that he valued exercising control unilaterally and did not value collegial, shared decision making. The staff members valued competition and avoiding criticism but not collegiality and assertiveness. This state of affairs was contrary to the values of the larger organization, which was undertaking a major initiative to promote inclusive decision making. It was also contrary to the professional and personal values of the staff members. Lab technologists are dedicated to contributing their analytical skills to improving the well-being of patients. Their social environment was getting in the way of their work. The people in the lab needed help to work in accordance with their values and those of the larger institution.

For Martha, the initial staff survey helped indicate the urgency of building community in her sector of the hospital. The survey results made it clear that her sense of distress was shared by other members of her work setting. That the survey was conducted at all served as a signal to Martha and her colleagues that the larger hospital organization was concerned with their personal perspectives and their emotional experience of their work. And it communicated to managers the importance the hospital placed on the sense of community within the various units of the larger organization.

In light of the survey results, a strategic task force focusing on the issue of community and collaboration in the hospital worked with Martha's unit to develop open, honest communication and respect. The lab's contribution to the hospital was assessed in terms of its sense of community as well as its technical performance. The priority on building community was made explicit to everyone involved in the unit.

For the people working there, the values clarification process made much more salient the core organizational value of collaboration and community. It helped the lab to develop a stronger sense of identity. It made people aware of their unique skills and perspectives, but also of the consistency between their values and those of their colleagues elsewhere in the hospital. Most importantly in this situation, it initiated a means of resolving several value conflicts among the people in that work setting:

- By voicing employees' perspective on the lab, the process let managers know that merely appearing to pursue the hospital's mission would not suffice. Management would no longer be assessed solely by superficial performance indicators but also by a direct assessment of staff members' experience.

- The outcome of the values clarification process in conjunction with the overall staff survey was to identify the lab as a setting that needed training and development in collaborative management.

- The values clarification process confirmed that employees could contribute to the overall functioning of the hospital by communicating openly and honestly.

Promoting Fairness

For Bill, the network manager at the university, the problem with unfairness stemmed from a different kind of value problem. His group worked consistently according to his values and those of the larger organization—the university's mission depended upon expertise and contributed to its development through education and research. But its salary system was inconsistent with this value because salary was determined by job category or seniority, not expertise. Moreover, Bill's expertise was constantly being discounted by people who had far less expertise but much more power. The innovation award was supposedly given for expertise, but it was perceived as hypocritical and mere hype in light of Bill's daily work experiences. Bill was looking for something more meaningful, for greater fairness, respect, and recognition for what he could do for the university, but the organization was not providing it.

For Bill, the initial survey provided a means of expressing his frustrations. However, he was impressed that the university used the occasion of the staff survey to show that fairness and respect were critical issues for it.

The values clarification process revealed inherent contradictions between the university's reliance on high-level expertise and its unwillingness to compensate people accordingly. The discussions of values and value conflicts within Bill's unit were a starting point for resolving conflicts between the organization's technological aspirations (as indicated by its innovation award) and its lack of responsiveness to the contributions of individuals in their day-to-day work.

Reducing Value Conflict

Steve's problem at the bank stemmed from a conflict between two of the bank's own values: maximizing cash flow and providing customer service. From Steve's perspective the bank's policy emphasized cash flow at the expense of customer service. It interfered with his capacity as a staff member to do his best in the long run for both the bank and its clientele. This policy reduced his effectiveness by restricting the extent to which he could use his judgment in resolving value conflicts, and it reduced his feeling of engagement with work by de-emphasizing the value of customer service to which he was deeply committed.

Steve felt that the staff survey gave central management a picture of the uneven impact of its policies on the diverse branch offices. The problems that employees communicated through the survey and the values clarification process highlighted the distinct perspective of Steve's branch. The acknowledgment of diversity across the branches balanced the emphasis on central values in a large organization. A specific focus on the four dimensions of customer service values allowed a more thorough consideration of the adverse impact of blanket policies on practices within specific branches. Ultimately, it gave small branches the authority to serve customers in the most effective manner.

The staff survey and values clarification process also provided an occasion for an open discussion of the bank's downsizing strategy. For management, it was an opportunity to state the rationale behind its decisions and to demonstrate how the strategy served the organization. For staff members who felt excluded or hurt by the downsizing process, it was an opportunity to present their point of view.

A NEW WORLD OF WORK

Throughout this book our focus has been on revitalizing life in a large organization. Large organizations continue to be where most of the action is, but events affecting them are not the only events happening in the world of work. While organizations are changing their approach to people during the current crisis, many people have lost patience and are opting for something altogether different. In other words, the world of work is changing for people as well as for organizations. Not everyone is content to wait around while organizations figure out what they're going to do.

Many young people graduating from high school today are thinking about something quite different than a traditional career. For many, work is a series of limited-term contracts, often with only a superficial connection among them. It has become increasingly rare to find a stable, ongoing job. This is a critical situation for many young people, but not for all.

A significant number of young people are showing a complete lack of interest in corporate life. They fail to see the attraction. From the outside, many large organizations appear to offer few opportunities to achieve something of significance. When organizations in the private and public sector left their values behind, they diminished their capacity to attract talented people. Many of these people want to make a meaningful contribution, but adding another point to a corporation's profit margin does not seem to be enough. At the same time, the staffing shortages, stagnant salaries, and declining professional standards of the public arena also offer a bleak image of organizational life. What could be so great about working in such a place?

Organizational life is apparently no more attractive once people get inside, and the problems often center on the mismatches between people and their jobs. Basically, when the organization has lost touch with people—when it ignores what they value, what they work for, and what they need—they may be motivated to leave the organization behind. Probably one of the best-known refugees from office life is cartoonist Scott Adams, creator of the *Dilbert* comic strip. Adams left his job of many years in a corporate cubicle and now earns millions poking fun at office life during the current crisis and its characteristic downsizing, cost containment, and corporate double-talk. And many of his zinging insights have to do with the clash between economic and human values.

Having tried office life and disliked it, many talented, educated people in their twenties have similarly left well-paying positions in established firms to strike out on their own. As one woman said about her departure from a small independent consulting group, "Hey, I know this is risky, but do you think staying with this job isn't? This corporation lays off people all the time, regardless of how good they are or what they have contributed over the years."

But even if corporate life is no longer secure, the alternative isn't necessarily more so. So just what is the appeal of striking out on your own? A big part of it comes back to values. People in their twenties today grew up in a society in which the expectation of a meaningful job seemed legitimate. From kindergarten to graduate school, the educational system has promoted the ideal of doing work that is enjoyable and important. The message has not only been repeated and modeled but will not be relinquished without a fight.

That goal is what the strategies we have discussed in this book aim to achieve. In the previous chapters we looked at two ways of changing organizations: from the perspective of individuals and from the perspective of organizations. Both approaches are risky— neither is a sure thing and both can even backfire, making things worse. In addition, both approaches entail a lot of work and take a long time to be successful. You need to be deeply committed to an organization in order even to embark on the process, let alone to see it through to completion. This commitment may be likely in people who have made a longtime career commitment to an organization, but it is not likely in every new staff member, especially those who are on short-term contracts that were specifically designed to give the organization staffing flexibility.

When people decide to opt out of organizational life, they put the priority on their values rather than on financial gain, just as we have been encouraging organizations to do. Although people may be uncertain about how they will obtain the capital and cash flow necessary to pay off student loans or buy a home, there are clear limits as to how much they will tolerate in order to pursue these ends.

> Kathy is a twenty-six-year-old employment counselor for a private firm that helps people with disabilities find jobs. A few years ago, she was sure that she would be admitted to the clinical graduate program of her choice after receiving an honors degree in psychology, but that did not pan out. After getting over the initial shock, she worked as a research assistant on a short-term contract before finding a permanent job with an employment firm. She had never imagined doing this kind of work, but her keen interest in people, self-confidence, and good basic education in psychology helped her to learn quickly. After three years she had earned a solid reputation with the company and its clientele. She was well positioned to advance within the company.
>
> But she didn't pursue it. Kathy's priority was to increase her education in order to have more control over her work. Without that degree, someone else always had the final word on what she did with her clients. She also wanted to be actively involved in research in order to understand more of the basic issues involved in her work. Her work situation could not develop into the role she wanted. So she left the job to obtain her degree and work as a counselor in private practice. She had a good idea of the perils that lay in this path, but her current job just was not enough.

Another group of people who are less than enthusiastic about committing to organizational change are those who have an opportunity for early retirement—usually with a long-term pension fund, at times supplemented by buyout packages. Freed from financial pressures and disenchanted with the diminishing emphasis on what they value within an organization, many people depart. Some see it as a long-awaited chance to distance themselves from work and to pursue personal goals. Others see it as an opportunity to concentrate on what they value in their work without the negative interference of organizational life. They can pursue these values without having to deal with the demands and risks of initiating organizational change.

> In his position as director of organizational development, Ted worked with a management team to bring a quality management approach to a large public urban hospital. But because of a change in government, strategic cost-reduction became the order of the day. The CEO was replaced by one with a different philosophy and a new management team. Ted was offered a more junior position providing support services during a significant downsizing process.
>
> This work was directly contrary to Ted's values. Although he had significant financial pressures—children approaching university age and a long-term mortgage—and was given only a modest cash settlement, he decided to leave the hospital and establish himself as an independent consultant specializing in group problem solving, planning, and quality management. Two years later, Ted has no regrets. The money is tight, the hours long, and the uncertainty immense, but he has confidence in his skills and in the long-term viability of his approach.

So there are alternatives to trying to fix an organization. They're not easy. They have their risks. And they are the best option for only some of the people some of the time. But they offer ways of working that are consistent with people's values, and they leave the ponderous weight of organizational life behind. The downside to this approach is that the world of organizations and their potential are often abandoned to unsympathetic hands. As we said at the beginning of this book, an organization is a work environment in which people can accomplish things that are greater than what they can do on their own. It's a means of contributing to the good of the larger community, although it also has the potential to cause significant damage to that community. Leaving organizational life may be the best decision for some people, but it may not be the best decision for society at large.

COMMUNITY IN A CHANGING WORKPLACE

During the current crisis, organizational missions and individual career orientations are changing and often conflicting. So it is not surprising that organizations often work at cross-purposes. They produce statements of their mission and goals that they cannot apply to their day-to-day operations. Instead of bringing about greater harmony and dedication, unfulfilled commitments to excellence produce cynicism and indifference. Despite the efforts and goodwill of a lot of people, the values embodied in missions are not driving management strategies. Few organizations can get past the immediate pressures of the current working world.

In the midst of so much conflict, it's hard to have a sense of working together. The perception of self-interest in one area of an organization prompts others to put their self-interest first and foremost too. As more employees adopt this stance, an organization becomes fragmented. People in one area cannot comprehend the principles or motives of their colleagues elsewhere in the organization. The lack of common purpose undermines the organization as a community.

Is this erosion of community a serious loss? Absolutely. People have always looked for a sense of community at work. They have been pleased when it is present and disappointed when it is absent. A job without at least one supportive collegial relationship is unbearably lonely. Engagement with work requires a person's full participation in the social environment of the workplace. The support, recognition, and collaboration of others in the job environment permit people to focus their energy effectively, justify their involvement, and extend their achievements—in other words, a strong organizational community prevents burnout.

Is a sense of community too idealistic a goal in this day and age? We don't think so. And our top candidate for building such community is shared values. Not a vague and noble-sounding mission statement from on high, but some grassroots endorsement of the things that make the job most meaningful and important. Whether articulated within a particular work group or throughout the organization as a whole, truly shared values can be the most cohesive element in the work setting. We hope that the values clarification process we presented in this chapter may be the first step in building the kind of job environment that will restore this crucial sense of engagement at work.

Afterword: Moving Toward a Better Future

When an organizational environment is unresponsive to people—to their aspirations, their limitations, and the way they work—chronic burnout is the inevitable result. What we have argued throughout this book is that it's time to put a higher priority on human values in the workplace. Human values are not a luxury but a necessity if we are to get through the current crisis and move successfully into the future. As we've shown, it is far too costly to tolerate the erosion of burnout. The only alternative, for both economic and humane reasons, is to build engagement with work.

SIX PATHS TO ENGAGEMENT

Several roads lead to greater harmony between people and their jobs—in fact, there are six of them. The six areas of organizational life in which mismatches occur are the immediate environment people encounter at work, and within each of these areas are the starting points for the journey from burnout to engagement. Each of these six areas contains the critical factors that either cause the problems of mismatch and burnout or offer the solutions of good fit and engagement. These factors either contribute to exhaustion or sustain the energy that people bring to their work. They either cause cynicism and alienation or promote increased involvement and commitment to the job. They either produce a lack of accomplishment and inadequacy or lead to greater effectiveness and achievement.

Any of the six mismatches provides a good starting point for moving toward the goal of a better life at work. If we look at them in terms of fit and engagement rather than mismatch and burnout they are translated into the following guideposts:

- Sustainable workload
- Feelings of choice and control
- Recognition and reward
- A sense of community
- Fairness, respect, and justice
- Meaningful and valued work

Along each of the six paths toward these goals, there are two challenges: (1) creating harmony between people and their jobs in a way that leads to (2) changing the job environment as well as the people. Targeting the job is critical, given all the evidence that burnout and engagement are primarily a function of the job situation. People cannot bear the entire burden of adjusting to fit the job, particularly when their efforts at that adjustment hit the upper limits and still fail to bridge the gap. Effective solutions need to recognize and accommodate both sides of the mismatch between job and person.

It is for this reason that the change processes outlined in Chapters Five and Six involve *both* the person and the organization. Lasting progress, no matter which of the six paths it started from, will depend on mutual effort and shared agreement, no matter what the specific solution may be. However, progress does *not* depend on developing cumbersome bureaucratic procedures and structures to combat burnout. The challenge for organizational management is to find ways to increase engagement without weighing themselves down with an increased administrative burden.

Picking the Best Path

So where to begin? Which path is likely to lead to the greatest success? Which is the easiest to pursue, or the least costly? Unfortunately, there are no simple answers to those questions. It just depends. Specifically, it depends on the following:

- The nature of the job
- The characteristics of the organization and the work group
- The external factors affecting the organization

For example, control and autonomy may be particularly important issues for people who have been trained to use their professional judgment but are now operating under a tight system of micromanagement. This was the situation that Stan and his therapist colleagues faced, as we described in Chapters One and Five. In other occupations, issues of control may be less large but issues of reward may be more critical. Clearly, this was the case for John and his fellow teachers. If teamwork and collaboration are central to doing the job, then issues of community and conflict may be especially significant. In organizations facing external pressures to cut budgets and downsize, workload is likely to be the area in which the mismatch is greatest.

Therefore, the choice of path should rest on two key questions: Which area of mismatch is causing the greatest problems? Which area has the greatest potential to lead to change?

As we noted in Chapter Six, a staff survey can be a useful tool in generating an answer to these questions. But it's important to realize that the answer may not be the same for both questions. Sometimes the mismatch may be large but the options for dealing with it few. A common example, particularly during the current crisis, is work overload—fewer people are being asked to do more under economic circumstances that don't permit a redeployment of resources to address the problem.

The best path to take is to choose a mismatch of major—not of trivial—concern whose resolution has the potential to generate and allow implementation of concrete solutions. However, the actual choice may not be as critical as you might think. Remember our discussion of the change processes in Chapters Five and Six—carrying out the process itself affects related mismatches. For example, a strategy that focuses on resolving reward issues (as in the case of John and the other school teachers) may also help clarify values, improve fairness of procedures, and promote a sense of community. The bottom line is that the act of starting down a path is more important than which path you choose. In a sense all six paths eventually link up and lead to the same destination.

Balancing Mismatches

A perfect fit between person and job translates into perfect harmony in all six areas of mismatch. The reality for many people likely falls short of that ideal, but that doesn't mean the reality is intolerable. Even if there are mismatches in some areas, their negative effects may be offset by greater harmony in others. So it may not be necessary to deal with all the mismatches, just some of them. A vivid example of this balancing act can be found in the story of the computer software company that follows.

A large number of employees were hired to work on the design and implementation of a major project for a national computer software company. They had to commit themselves to a minimum of five years on the project, and during that time their workload was easily eighty hours a week. They literally worked night and day, and they had little time to spend with their families or friends. A major mismatch in work overload? You bet. Big burnout as a result? No way. This surprised a number of people, but not us, because when we looked at the other five areas, we found good fit and high engagement:

- The employees were given a great deal of control over their work on the project, and they valued this autonomy highly.

- The monetary rewards for the project were potentially enormous once the five years were completed successfully. (And in fact some people retired immediately afterward as millionaires.)

- The project team, as well as the company as a whole, had a strong sense of camaraderie and community—they were a special group accomplishing very special things.

- The rules governing the commitment to the project were fair and clear from the outset—"We're going to own your life for the next five years but if you do well you'll be rich and free to do whatever you want"—and the company made good on those promises.

- Everyone bought into the explicit values and vision of the company's leadership that their innovations in computer technology would change the world and make it a better place.

Although this particular example is not a typical one, the point should be clear: a balance between mismatches is what's most critical. People may be very willing to work long hours and do extra work *if* they feel rewarded and respected for it, or if the work is especially meaningful to them. In contrast, if there is a lot of conflict within the organization and a lack of fairness, then people may be unwilling to endure high overload or low rewards.

It's impossible to say which patterns of mismatches are more easily tolerated by workers in the workplace. But our research has led us to make a few observations.

First, it is common belief that there is just one dimension to job stress, work overload. Indeed, overload is often considered to be a synonym for stress. But in our burnout model, overload is only one of six mismatches in the workplace. And it's not always the most critical, especially if things are going well in some of the other areas.

Second, when jobs are scaled back to part-time, short-term, temporary, or contract positions, then the dominant mismatches become breakdown in community and absence of fairness—and as a result, the importance of material rewards increases dramatically.

Third, for jobs that are more long-term, the primary concerns are likely to be with values and fairness. No matter what else, people have to judge the job as meaningful and worthy of a full commitment of their time and effort.

A CALL TO ACTION

The time has come to recognize the truth about burnout—it takes an emotional toll on the worker and it takes an economic toll on the workplace. And the time has come to start taking new action to prevent burnout and to build engagement.

The new action that we are advocating involves the job environment, not just the person. People cannot continue to ignore the powerful influence that the social context exerts on individual behavior. But neither can they assume that it is so powerful that any attempts to change it are useless. We believe that the gaps between the person and the job *can* be bridged in a way that reintroduces human values into the workplace and makes it more responsive to people.

Now we have given you the tools you need to beat burnout and enhance engagement:

- You know what burnout is, its three dimensions, its causes, and its consequences.
- You know the six mismatches that are the key sources of burnout, and the paths that lead away from them and toward engagement.
- You know the key steps involved in the two processes of change.

- You know the survey measures that are available to facilitate the change process at the organizational level.

But simply having the tools is not enough. You also need a great deal of patience and a commitment to keep the process on track. Progress will be slow, not fast. Much as we would like to be able to offer quick and easy solutions—the equivalent of "Take two aspirin, get a good night's sleep, and you'll be fine"—the hard truth is that there are no simple answers to the complex problem of burnout.

But there are answers, and that is what this book is all about. The answers have to do with building productive engagement with work and with reducing the mismatches between people and their jobs. With patience and persistence on the part of both individuals and the organization, progress can be made toward the healthier and more humane workplace of the future.

Appendix: Assessing the Work Environment

An organizational survey process can help assess the impact of major organizational initiatives on employees. The results of such a survey indicate the range of views staff members have on critical issues. They show the areas in which the organization is doing well compared with similar organizations and those where it is encountering more difficulty than usual. This information lets the organization know its current state of affairs.

THE MASLACH BURNOUT INVENTORY: MEASURING PERSONAL EXPERIENCE

The Maslach Burnout Inventory (MBI) is the definitive measure of burnout, used by organizations and by researchers to assess how employees experience their work. It is a reliable questionnaire that provides a concise perspective on the energy, involvement, and effectiveness of staff members on the job.

There are three versions of the MBI. The original Human Services Survey is most appropriate for service providers. A slightly modified Educators Survey focuses on the teaching profession. A more recent addition is the General Survey, which is applicable to people in a wide range of occupations. The latter differs from the other two versions in that it does not refer to the service relationship with recipients. Rather, it emphasizes the respondents' relationship to the work in general.

The MBI measures the three core dimensions of a person's experience with work: exhaustion-energy; depersonalization-involvement; and inefficacy-accomplishment. The scale items are rated on a 7-point frequency scale ranging from 0 (*never*) and 1 (*a few times a year or less*) to 5 (*a few times a week*) and 6 (*daily*). Work groups that score high on Emotional Exhaustion and Depersonalization and low on Personal Accomplishment are experiencing burnout. Those with the opposite pattern—scoring low on Emotional Exhaustion and Depersonalization and high on Personal Accomplishment—are experiencing many aspects of engagement with work.

The MBI focuses on people's personal experience of work. The dominant structure for the items is a statement of a feeling (for example, emotionally drained, callous, exhilarated) that is attributed to work. The attribution process is a defining quality of burnout. The close association between burnout and work differentiates it from more general emotional states, such as depression, which pervade every aspect of life without being tied to a specific domain of life. Thus, the MBI assesses burnout as the result of problems at work, not as a psychiatric syndrome.

Managers and researchers use the MBI with other inventories in order to establish the relationship between burnout and organizational policies, productivity, or social support. This work has led to a wealth of research, which is summarized in the third edition of the *Maslach Burnout Inventory Manual* (Maslach, Jackson, and Leiter, 1996).

THE STAFF SURVEY: LISTENING TO COMPLEX ORGANIZATIONS

One of the most productive complements to the MBI is the Staff Survey, which we introduced in Chapter Six as a means of planning and assessing organizational interventions intended to build engagement with work.

The Staff Survey developed through a collaborative effort in which a university research team at the Center for Organizational Research and Development of Acadia University in Wolfville, Nova Scotia, led by Michael Leiter, worked with organizational managers and service providers. Both the researchers and the managers wanted a way of taking a snapshot of what occurs in organizations that are undergoing major change. The researchers wanted to assess the impact of organizational change on people; the managers wanted practical solutions for the problems of providing leadership through these transitions.

The answers to both questions lie in three basic domains: (1) employees' personal experience of working in the organization (including the burnout-engagement continuum); (2) the six areas of organizational life (where mismatches can occur); and (3) the management of that organizational environment. The Staff Survey provides a picture of how these three domains connect with one another as an organization responds to either external change or changes brought about on its own initiative.

The Staff Survey measures staff members' perceptions of the organization, their relationship with the job, and their personal experience at work. Within each of these broad areas are specific focus issues. Together, the components of the Staff Survey in conjunction with the Maslach Burnout Inventory describe the management environment, the six areas of organizational life, and staff members' experience of their work. The result is a framework for planning change.

The Management Environment

The section on the management environment measures eight areas of management policy and activity in the organization.

Perceptions of Change	Whether things are getting better or worse
Mission and Goals	How the organization's goals and mission affect work

Management	How well central management is addressing demands
Supervision	Employees' perceptions of their immediate supervisor
Communication	How staff receive information about the organization
Performance Appraisal	Performance appraisal procedures at the organization
Health and Safety	Threats to health, career, or well-being
Work and Home	The impact of one domain on the other

Most of the items on the survey are rated on a 5-point scale ranging from 1 (*strongly disagree*) to 5 (*strongly agree*). A few of the scales use a frequency scale, such as the one used with the MBI items, or other scales appropriate to the items' wording.

Here are some sample items:

Perceptions of Change	Over the past six months the quality of service in this organization has improved.
Mission and Goals	The organization's goals influence my day-to-day work activities.
Management	From my point of view, management delegates appropriate authority to staff.
Supervision	From my point of view, my immediate supervisor encourages innovative/creative thinking about improving quality.
Communication	My sources of information about the organization are usually accurate.
Performance Appraisal	The feedback from my last performance appraisal was beneficial.
Health and Safety	When at work, I am at risk of verbal abuse from service recipients.
Work and Home	My work demands interfere with my personal life.

In the assessment of change, staff members indicate whether they see things improving or getting worse in key areas of organizational life. The central area of concern here is the quality of products or services: Has it been getting better or worse over the previous six months? The analysis considers specific areas of change, such as quality, staff morale, or involvement in decision making, as well as staff members' overall assessment of change.

The Mission and Goals section assesses staff members' awareness of the organization's mission and goals as well as their impact on the day-to-day work. In the Management section and the Supervisor section, staff members give their views on the performance of the organization's central and immediate management. By asking some of the same questions about both levels of management, the survey can spot where staff members are running into conflict with management and where they are finding support and encouragement. The Communications section assesses the organization's capacity to exchange timely, accurate, and relevant information. The Performance Appraisal section asks how recently staff members participated in a performance appraisal and whether they found the experience to be of value. An assessment of these six areas together indicates what it is like to be on the receiving end of management policies in the organization.

Health and Safety looks at physical hazards (for example, interactions with equipment; poor air quality), microbiological hazards (for example, customers with colds; patients with hepatitis), performance hazards (back injury from lifting), social hazards (verbal abuse; sexual harassment), and career hazards (dead-end jobs; job loss). The analysis identifies occupational groups or sites that are especially vulnerable as well as those that are successfully managing these hazards. The Center for Organizational Research and Development has developed the Workplace Hazards Assessment Measure (WHAM) from a model that defines risk as increasing with the prevalence and lethality of the hazard, and decreasing with the control that staff members gain over the hazard through training and experience. This model was successful in assessing occupational risk among aircraft maintenance technicians, for example. WHAM permits a detailed examination of staff issues surrounding problems with a hazardous work environment.

Work and Family provides a brief assessment of the interaction between work and family. It looks at the potential for interference as well as for mutual support. This section recognizes that staff members have many dimensions to their lives beyond work. It considers the boundary of the management environment: To what extent are outside demands intruding on organizational life? To what extent is organizational life interfering with staff members' personal lives?

The Six Areas of Organizational Life

The next section of the Staff Survey measures the six areas of organizational life, providing indicators of mismatches or harmony.

Workload	Extent to which demands are manageable or overwhelming
Control	Amount of control people feel in their jobs
Reward	The effectiveness of rewards and recognition systems
Community	The organization's responsiveness to staff and community
Fairness	Respect and fairness among people in the organization
Values	Personal and organizational values about work

The following are examples of sample items:

Workload	This job demands more than I can fit into a work day.
Control	I am my own boss when it comes to pursuing the tasks that I am assigned.

Reward	The recognition and reward people receive reflect their contribution to the organization.
Community	This organization does a good job of responding to the distinct cultural perspectives of its client population.
Fairness	Respect is evident in relationships within the organization.
Values	This job provides me with opportunities to do work that I feel is important.

The survey items make a clear differentiation among the various areas; for example, they determine whether the organization is experiencing primarily a problem in workload, control, or a combination of the two. The values section offers an opportunity for staff members to express the important values they bring to their work and to contrast these with what they perceive to be the organization's values. This section of the survey provides a clear view on the six mismatches that we have discussed in this book.

Personal Experiences

Staff members complete the Maslach Burnout Inventory in conjunction with the Staff Survey. Their overall responses to the MBI indicate the organization's place on the continuum from burnout to engagement with distinct assessments of each of burnout's three components of energy, involvement, and effectiveness.

Energy	Level of emotional, creative, or physical energy.
Involvement	Degree of concern or cynicism about work.
Effectiveness	The impact of work on personal accomplishment.

The following are sample items:

Emotional Exhaustion	I feel emotionally drained from my work.
Depersonalization	I've become more callous toward people since I took this job.
Personal Accomplishment	I feel exhilarated after working closely with my recipients.

The Staff Survey considers two other areas of personal experience: physical symptoms that are often associated with stress (for example, headaches, stomach upsets, sleeplessness), and one's commitment to the organization and to one's profession. These aspects of personal experience are related to the continuum from burnout to engagement.

Physical Symptoms	Health problems associated with job stress
Commitment	Dedication to organizational goals and to one's occupation

The following are sample items:

Physical Symptoms	How often do you experience sleeplessness?
Commitment	I feel content with the profession or occupation I have chosen for myself.

Open-Ended Questions

An open-ended question at the end of the Staff Survey—"Please comment on any issue of importance to you regarding this organization"—supplements the survey with a distinct kind of information. Generally, 20 percent to 30 percent of staff members write a comment ranging from one line to many pages. In our surveys people have laid out clear plans for change in their area, expanded on the sections of the survey, pointed out important issues neglected by the survey, expressed frustration emphatically, and related instructive moral tales.

Analyzing the written comments for unique qualitative data can be hard work. We have found that the effort pays off, but it is time consuming and demanding. The earlier, more structured sections of the Staff Survey produce quantitative data that can be quickly scanned and analyzed. They provide an efficient way to process information from hundreds or thousands of people across an organization and provide them with feedback in a matter of weeks.

Processing the written comments takes longer. The comments are typed into a word processor, read by the research staff, and analyzed with a qualitative research program. This analysis produces an index of themes. A reader can look up an issue—such as performance appraisals—and find all of the comments pertaining to this area, noting its cross-references with other themes. The organization receives a volume containing an indexed copy of all comments. This is a valuable resource for people wanting to gain a deeper understanding of the issues behind the survey.

USING THE RESULTS

The initial survey assessment provides a baseline for assessing further progress toward organizational objectives. Follow-up surveys measure change, indicating where things are progressing well, where they are meeting with mixed success, and where progress is problematic.

The survey identifies the hot issues for an organization. It shows which aspects of the organizational environment are out of sync with similar organizations or with the aspirations of staff members. The relationships among the various measures in the survey show the leverage points. Although managers cannot directly influence the thoughts and feelings of people throughout the organization, they can change policies on decision making, establish professional development programs for supervisors, and restructure the workload. The survey indicates which management initiatives are likely to have the greatest beneficial impact on staff.

Critical Issues

Identifying the hot issues is a critical contribution of the survey. Managers have limited control over their areas of responsibility. Their areas are interlocked with other areas in the organization, so that every attempt at change becomes an occasion for interdepartmental negotiation. Furthermore, the big issues always involve people, all of whom have minds of their own. Attempts to improve organizational life are fraught with difficulties, as vulnerable to unforeseen and unwelcome consequences as they are likely to lead to successful outcomes. Managers have a limited number of opportunities to initiate change. Each failed initiative increases resistance to the next attempt from staff members, other parts of the organization, or central management. Unsuccessful change initiatives are expensive and cause inconvenience for many people. So it is important to get it right.

Three outcomes of the Staff Survey help managers to get it right. First, the analysis looks at the relationship between the three core dimensions of burnout and the six areas of organizational life. This analysis highlights the hot issues for the organization, where the major mismatches and harmonies are. Second, the strong relationships between the six areas and organizational measures highlight the leverage points for management: What do managers control that has a meaningful impact on people? Third, the open-ended answers often suggest productive strategies for implementing change. They communicate ideas from the staff members who are doing the work. They indicate what the organization is prepared to tolerate in terms of change.

Work Group Profiles

In addition to a comprehensive report on the entire organization, the Staff Survey can be reported in terms of profiles on workgroups. These profiles indicate a work group's score on the staff's personal experience, the six areas of organizational life, and the management environment.

Figures A.1 and A.2 offer profiles of two hospital units. The dashes in the upper area of the profiles indicate the highest score of a unit in the hospital whereas the dashes in the lower area indicate the lowest score of a unit in the hospital. The bars in the graph indicate the average score of a work group on that measure. The overall average score for the entire hospital is on the zero line of this graph.

In the first example (see Figure A.1), the work group has problems with burnout, as indicated by high scores on Exhaustion and Cynicism and low scores on Efficacy. The scores on Symptoms and Commitment are close to the overall average. The six areas of organizational life suggest that the hot issues for this work group are reward and values. This group gave the most negative rating to these areas of any in the hospital. Workload and fairness received ratings that were slightly higher than the average, and community was rated lower than the average.

This analysis suggests that an intervention based solely on reducing workload would be unlikely to have much of an impact on the relationships these staff members have with their work. An initiative that targets reward and values is likely to be much more promising.

The assessment of the management environment suggests the appropriate leverage point for improving reward and values is the unit's relationship with the larger organization. The low ratings this group gave to organizational goals and to central management are in sharp contrast to its positive rating of immediate supervision and its indifferent ratings of other aspects of the management environment. The group appears to be experiencing a crisis in its relationship with the larger organization, with members of the work group attached to their own values and goals and in direct opposition to those of the larger organization. This pattern suggests that the nurse manager for this unit could be pivotal in any initiative to build engagement with work for this group.

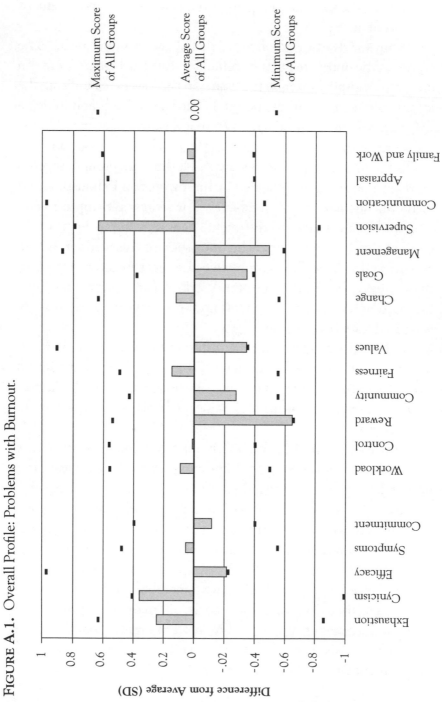

FIGURE A.1. Overall Profile: Problems with Burnout.

In the second example (see Figure A.2), the work group is engaged with their work, as indicated by low scores on Exhaustion and Cynicism and high scores on Efficacy. The group reports infrequent symptoms and strong commitment. The six areas of organizational life suggest that the hot issues for this work group are workload, control, fairness, and values. This group gave the most extreme rating of any group in the hospital to nearly all of these areas.

The assessment of the management environment includes a moderately positive rating of the organization's goals and a moderately critical view of management as well as a strong endorsement of the immediate supervisor and an optimistic view of change. Members of the unit feel well informed in comparison with their colleagues in other units in the hospital but express skepticism about the performance appraisal system, which is consistent with their indifferent rating of the organization's reward systems.

This unit can serve as an ideal in terms of staff member relationships with their work. It indicates the resilience of staff members—things do not have to be perfect to support engagement with work, but some areas are critical. It indicates that it is important for some key areas—workload, control, fairness, and values—to be in harmony with staff members.

The work group profiles of responses from the MBI and the Staff Survey create a picture of a group's crises and opportunities.

Process Objectives

The Staff Survey is designed to address concerns of staff members during the current crisis in the nature of work and the workplace. The process of voicing concerns and perceptions helps staff members participate more actively in the development of their work environment. Wide distribution of survey reports followed by open meetings and discussions on the issues can be a powerful catalyst in developing a stronger sense of community in a complex organization.

The work group profiles contribute to the empowerment of teams throughout the organization. They provide a sense of a single

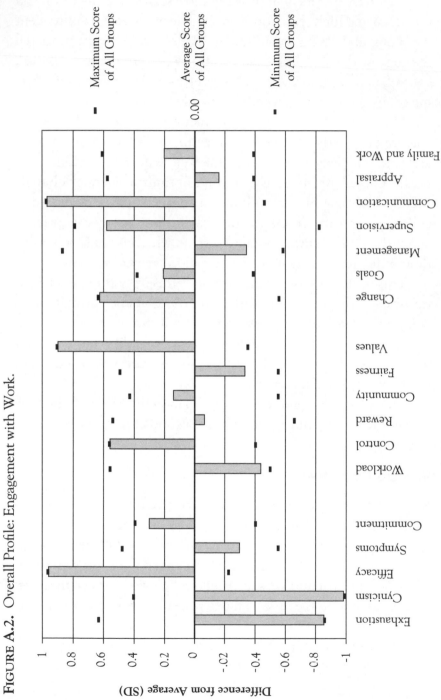

FIGURE A.2. Overall Profile: Engagement with Work.

unit within the broader context. Profile reports highlight values that units share with the larger organization and points on which they have a unique perspective. This is the kind of information that teams can use to address their problems and opportunities.

BIBLIOGRAPHY

Leiter, M. P., and Robichaud, L. "Relationships of Occupational Hazards with Burnout: An Assessment of Measures and Models." *Journal of Occupational Health Psychology*, 1997, *2*, 1–11.

Leiter, M. P., and Schaufeli, W. B. "Consistency of the Burnout Construct Across Occupations." *Anxiety, Stress, and Coping*, 1996, *9*, 229–243.

Maslach, C., Jackson, S. E., and Leiter, M. P. (1996). *The Maslach Burnout Inventory*. (3rd ed.) Palo Alto, Calif.: Consulting Psychologists Press.

For further information on the MBI, contact:
Consulting Psychologists Press
3803 East Bayshore Road
P.O. Box 10096
Palo Alto, California 94303
Tel.: 1–800–624–1765
Fax: 1–650–969–8608
www.cpp-db.com

For further information on the Staff Survey, contact:
The Center for Organizational Research and Development
Acadia University
Wolfville, Nova Scotia, Canada B0P 1X0
Tel: 1–902–585–1671
Fax: 1–902–585–3323
http://ace.acadiau.ca/science/cor/home.html

Endnotes

1. *Los Angeles Times*, Sept. 24, 1996.
2. *Herald-Journal* (Spartanburg, S.C.), Feb. 10, 1996.
3. *San Francisco Examiner*, Feb. 2, 1994.
4. Phillips, K. *Boiling Point: Democrats, Republicans, and the Decline of Middle-Class Prosperity*. New York: Random House, 1993, p. 196.
5. Gephardt, R., and Obey, D. "Downsizing the American Dream: A Staff Report of the House Democratic Policy Committee." [http://www.house.gov/democrats/research/downsize.html]. March 11, 1996.
6. Anderson, S., and Cavanaugh, J. "CEOs Win, Workers Lose: How Wall Street Rewards Job Destroyers." *The Institute for Policy Studies' Third Annual Analysis of Executive Compensation*. Washington, D.C.: The Institute for Policy Studies, 1996.
7. Appelbaum, E., Berg, P., and Baker, D. "The Economic Case for Corporate Responsibility to Workers." Economic Policy Institute Issue Brief no. 111. Cambridge, Mass.: The Electronic Policy Network, 1996.
8. Crystal, G. C. *In Search of Excess: The Overcompensation of American Executives*. New York: Norton, 1992.
9. Some of these cases were adapted from Yandrick, R. M. *Behavioral Risk Management: How to Avoid Preventable Losses from Mental Health Problems in the Workplace*. San Francisco: Jossey-Bass, 1996.

For Further Reading

The following references provide a fuller explication of the theory and research on which our book is based. In the first section, we describe the most recent source materials, beginning with our own work and then those of colleagues. In the second section, we provide a list of a variety of earlier books on the topic of burnout.

Schaufeli, W., Maslach, C., and Marek T. (eds.). *Professional Burnout: Recent Developments in Theory and Research*. Washington, D.C.: Taylor & Francis, 1993.

The chapters in this edited volume were written by an international group of the leading scholars on burnout. They present an array of theoretical perspectives on burnout, discuss the state of current research, and suggest directions for future scholarly work.

Maslach, C., Jackson, S. E., and Leiter, M. P. *Maslach Burnout Inventory Manual* (3rd ed.). Palo Alto, Calif.: Consulting Psychologists Press, 1996.

For those interested in burnout research, this manual summarizes the current empirical findings and outlines future directions for further study.

Cherniss, C. *Beyond Burnout*. New York: Routledge, 1995.

This book presents individual case studies of a group of human services professionals, who had first been interviewed ten years earlier. The author discusses key factors that seem to have been important for those who overcame burnout and for those who didn't.

Kleiber, D., and Enzmann, D. *Burnout: An International Bibliography*. Göttingen, Germany: Hogrefe, 1990.

This reference book lists all studies and articles on burnout published in the 1970s and 1980s. It contains a brief summary of this literature (in both English and German).

Potter, B. *Beating Job Burnout: How to Transform Work Pressure into Productivity*. Berkeley, Calif.: Ronin Publishing, 1993.
Potter, B. *Finding a Path with a Heart: How to Go from Burnout to Bliss*. Berkeley, Calif.: Ronin Publishing, 1995.

The two Potter publications are self-help books that draw on the workshops conducted by the author. The focus is on individual strategies for coping with burnout, and both books contain lots of exercises, drawings, stories, cartoons, and quotes.

EARLIER BOOKS

Cedoline, A. J. *Job Burnout in Public Education*. New York: Teachers College Press, 1982.

Cherniss, C. *Professional Burnout in Human Service Organizations*. New York: Praeger, 1980a.

Cherniss, C. *Staff Burnout: Job Stress in the Human Services*. Thousand Oaks, Calif.: Sage, 1980b.

Edelwich, J., with Brodsky, A. *Burnout: Stages of Disillusionment in the Helping Professions*. New York: Human Sciences Press, 1980.

Farber, B. A. (ed.). *Stress and Burnout in the Human Service Professions*. New York: Pergamon, 1983.

Freudenberger, H. J., and Richelson, G. *Burnout: The High Cost of High Achievement*. Garden City, N.Y.: Doubleday, 1980.

Gold, Y., and Roth, R. A. *Teachers Managing Stress and Preventing Burnout*. Bristol, Pa.: Falmer Press, 1993.

Golembiewski, R. T., and Munzenrider, R. F. *Phases of Burnout: Developments in Concepts and Applications*. New York: Praeger, 1988.

Golembiewski, R. T., Munzenrider, R. F., and Stevenson, J. G. *Stress in Organizations: Toward a Phase Model of Burnout*. New York: Praeger, 1986.

Jones, J. W. (ed.). *The Burnout Syndrome*. Park Ridge, Ill.: London House Press, 1983.

Maslach, C. *Burnout: The Cost of Caring*. Englewood Cliffs, N.J.: Prentice Hall, 1982.

McConnell, E. A. (ed.). *Burnout in the Nursing Profession*. St. Louis: Mosby, 1982.

Paine, W. S. (ed.). *Job Stress and Burnout*. Thousand Oaks, Calif.: Sage, 1982.

Pines, A., and Aronson, E. *Career Burnout: Causes and Cures*. New York: Free Press, 1988.

Pines, A., Aronson, E., and Kafry, D. *Burnout: From Tedium to Personal Growth*. New York: Free Press, 1981.

Veninga, R. L., and Spradley, J. P. *The Work/Stress Connection: How to Cope with Job Burnout*. Boston: Little, Brown, 1981.

Wessells, D. T., Kutscher, A. H., Seeland, I. B., Selder, F. E., Cherico, D. J., and Clark, E. J. (eds.). *Professional Burnout in Medicine and the Helping Professions*. New York: Haworth Press, 1989.

About the Authors

CHRISTINA MASLACH is professor of psychology at the University of California, Berkeley, where she has been on the faculty since 1971. She is best known as one of the pioneering researchers on job burnout and the author of the Maslach Burnout Inventory (MBI), the most widely used research measure in the burnout field. She has conducted research in a number of areas within social and health psychology.

In addition to writing numerous articles, Maslach has worked on books including *Burnout: The Cost of Caring* and the co-edited volume *Professional Burnout: Recent Developments in Theory and Research*. In recognition of these research accomplishments, the American Association for the Advancement of Science made her a Fellow, honoring her "For groundbreaking work on the applications of social psychology to contemporary problems." She was president of the Western Psychological Association, and won the Distinguished Teaching Award from the University of California at Berkeley. Recently, the American Psychological Association recognized her expertise as both a researcher and teacher by selecting her to deliver the prestigious G. Stanley Hall Lecture at its annual convention.

Maslach received her A.B., magna cum laude, in social relations from Harvard-Radcliffe College, and her Ph.D. in psychology from Stanford University.

Maslach's academic career was actually her second choice; she originally intended to become a professional dancer. She maintains her passion for the performing and fine arts and tries to keep her life filled with as much theater and music as possible.

MICHAEL P. LEITER is professor of psychology and dean of the faculty of science at Acadia University in Canada. He is director of the Center for Organizational Research and Development, which applies high-quality research methods to human resource issues confronting organizations. He developed the Staff Survey for assessing the way people perceive complex organizations. This approach to organizational life arose from his extensive work with organizations that are undergoing major organizational change in North America and Europe. His research, which has received consistent financial support from the Social Sciences and Humanities Research Council of Canada, is published in major psychological and management journals.

He received his B.A. degree in psychology from Duke University, his M.A. from Vanderbilt University, and his Ph.D. from the University of Oregon. He teaches courses on organizational psychology and on stress at Acadia University. The research center provides a lively bridge between university studies and organizational consultation for himself and his students.

One of Leiter's major interests outside of organizational life is music. He plays baroque flute and Celtic music with friends in Nova Scotia, and he believes that fine music has a lot in common with harmonious organizational life.

Index

109–110, 122, 123–124, 135; crisis intervention versus, 80–81; employees and, 106–108, 109–115, 118–126; engagement and, 77, 102–105, 120, 148–153; goal orientation and, 103; human values promotion and, 128–147; initiating, 105–106; management and, 103–106, 107, 110–111, 113, 115, 116–118, 121–124; Maslach Burnout Inventory (MBI) and, 112, 155–156, 161–162, 169; as ongoing process, 22, 109, 110, 116, 125–126; organizational approach to, 103–127, 149, 153; problem-solving process and, 79–81, 103–127; staff surveys and, 107, 109–115, 119–125, 135–137, 139–141, 156–169; task forces and, 114–115, 118–119, 120–124, 125–126, 139; time required for, 115–116, 154; work groups and, 108, 111, 114, 115. See also Intervening in burnout

Pride, 13, 19, 28, 29–30

Problem-solving process: burnout intervention and, 79–99; burnout prevention and, 79–81, 103–127

Process: burnout intervention as ongoing, 80–81, 87–88, 92–93, 98–99; burnout prevention as ongoing, 22, 109, 110, 116, 125–126

Productivity: burnout and, 19, 33, 61, 64, 65–69, 74; burnout intervention and, 74–75; community breakdown and, 51–52; materialistic view and, 48; power redistribution and, 6–7; technology and, 5–6; workload and, 38–39. See also Work overload

Professional development, 48, 49, 57

Promotions, 15, 46–47. See also Performance appraisal

Psychiatric disorder: burnout as, 32, 33, 34, 156

Q

Quality: burnout and, 19, 65; burnout intervention and, 74–75, 91; burnout prevention and, 77, 102, 117–118, 119–126; cost cutting and, 57; lack of control and, 14; staff surveys and, 119–125; value conflict and, 55, 57; work overload and, 11

Quality management task force, 118, 119, 122–123

Quitting jobs: burnout and, 74, 81. See also Opting out of organizational life

R

Ramos, P., 124–125

Reagan administration, 46

Relationships. See Community; Community breakdown; Family issues; Friends

Remuneration. See Pay

Respect: benefit of, 78, 95; burnout prevention and, 139; lack of, 14, 15, 26, 27–28, 49, 52–53, 68, 96. See also Fairness; Self-respect

Restructuring. See Downsizing

Retaliation, 27–28, 68

Retirement: early, 144–145

Rewards: burnout prevention and, 122–123, 150–153; gaining more, 93–99, 123, 150–153; inequity of, 54, 68; insufficient, 12–13, 26, 27, 44–48, 67; interrelationship with other burnout causes, 92, 98, 125, 150–153; management and, 104; measuring (staff survey), 112–115, 122–123, 160, 161, 165, 167

S

Sabotage, 28

Safety: measuring workplace conditions for, 158, 159–160

Salaries. See Pay

Sartelli, W., 121–122

Satisfaction. See Job satisfaction

Scapegoating, 27

Scott Paper, 8

Security. See Job security

Self-confidence: loss of, 18, 19, 20, 27

Self-employment, 142–145

Self-improvement, 79

Self-respect: loss of, 15, 16–17

Signs of burnout, 17–18, 23–37; measuring, 156, 161–162. See also Causes of burnout; Cynicism; Exhaustion; Ineffectiveness

Sleep disturbances, 19, 42

Social dysfunction: burnout as, 18, 21, 28–32, 34, 37, 70–72

Social interaction. See Community

Social isolation: technology and, 14, 55, 56. See also Community breakdown; Detachment

Social security taxes, 46

Software designers, 73

Soul: erosion of, 17–21

Staff surveys: analyzing, 163; burnout prevention and, 107, 109–115, 135–137, 139–141; case study of, 119–126; description of, 156–163; hot issue identification and, 163–164; Maslach Burnout Inventory (MBI) and, 112, 155–156, 161–162, 169; using the results of, 163–169; work group profiles and, 164–169

Stealing, 28, 32, 68

Strategies: organizational, 57–59, 69

Stress management: individual approaches to, 62–63, 64–65, 70–72

Strikes: public sector, 45

Sunbeam, 4

Surveys. See Staff surveys

Symptoms of burnout. See Signs of burnout

T

Task forces: burnout prevention and, 114–115, 118–119, 120–124, 125–126, 139

Taxes: increase in, 46

Teachers: benefits of addressing burnout in, 73; burnout intervention and, 70–72, 93–99; burnout risk and, 20; community breakdown and, 26; engagement erosion and, 24–26; loss of control by, 7, 26; organizational strains and, 35–36; reward insufficiency and, 12–13, 25, 26, 93–99, 133; technology and, 5–6; unfairness and, 26; value conflict and, 19, 25, 26; work overload and, 12, 25, 26, 35, 41

Teamwork: loss of, 30, 47–48, 49, 50–51, 67–68; organizational intervention and, 75–76. See also Work groups

Technology: jobs replaced by, 3, 5–6; social isolation and, 14, 55, 56

Tension, 10, 19, 26, 30, 35–37, 42

Texas Instruments, 4

Textile industry, 4

Theft, 28, 32, 68

Thornhill, F., 118–119

Time: burnout intervention requires, 82; burnout prevention requires, 115–116, 154; work, increase in, 5, 40–41

Trust: burnout and, 14, 15, 27–28, 29, 44, 52–53, 54, 68; burnout intervention

and, 78; burnout prevention and, 135, 139

U

Ulcers, 42

Unions, 6–7, 40, 45, 67, 100, 124, 126

V

Value conflict: burnout and, 16–17, 26, 55–59, 69, 130, 133, 136, 138–141; burnout prevention and, 104, 108–109, 134–140, 150–153; customer service and, 16, 55–57, 58, 69, 136; interrelationship with other burnout causes, 87, 92, 98, 125, 150–153; management and, 16, 55, 104, 132, 133, 138–139, 140–141; measuring values (staff survey), 112–115, 124–125, 135–137, 160, 161, 165, 167; mission statements and, 57, 58–59, 69, 130–133, 146; resolving, 87, 134, 138, 139–141. See also Conflict; Economic values versus human values; Values

Values: attracting talented employees and, 142–144; clarifying, 133–141; community and, 136–147; discrepancies between actions and, 131–133; early retirement and, 144–145; human, promoting, 128–147; independent consulting and, 145; measuring (staff survey), 112–115, 124–125, 135–137, 160, 161, 165, 167; mission statements and, 130–133, 138; putting to use, 138–141. See also Economic values versus human values; Value conflict

W

Wages. See Pay

Weakness: burnout as, 21, 32, 34

Withdrawal. See Detachment

Work groups: burnout intervention and, 82–83, 84–85; burnout prevention and, 108, 111, 114, 115; conflict in, emotions and, 51–52; profiles on, 164–169; staff surveys and, 111; values clarification and, 137, 138. See also Teamwork

Work overload: bottom line and, 65–66; burnout and, 10–11, 15, 23, 26,